www.funwithcomposers.com

www.funwithcomposers.com

Fun with Composers

Composers

A Simple, Fun Approach to Classical music

Teacher's Guide

AGES 7-12

BY DEBORAH ZIOLKOSKI

Fun with Composers 7–12
Copyright © 2006 Fun with Composers

Fun with Composers
1541-134 A Street
Surrey, B.C.
Canada V4A 5P7
Fax: 604 541 2928
E-mail: *info@funwithcomposers.com*
www.funwithcomposers.com

Printed in Canada

Library and Archives Canada
Cataloguing in Publication

Ziolkoski, Deborah Lyn, 1968–
Fun with composers. Teacher's guide, ages 7–12 / author, Deborah Lyn Ziolkoski ; illustrator, Jim Fee.

ISBN 0-9780360-1-8
ISMN 0-9001385-1-4

1. School music--Instruction and study.
2. Music--Instruction and study--
Outlines, syllabi, etc. I. Title.

MT10.Z797 2006   372.87'044   C2006-901024-2

Cover Page Design
Eric Olson, *www.gallereo.com*

Music Maps and Composer Images
Jim Fee, *www.jimfee.ca*

Editor
Heidi Groschler

Design
Solo Corps, *www.solocorps.com*

Voice Performance
Corena Akeson, *cakeson@shaw.ca*

Recording Engineer
Jeff Tymoschuk, *jeff@greenwiremusic.com*

DVD
Jason Fredrickson, www.*reelmemories.biz*

Our Mission

The purpose of *Fun with Composers* is to spark excitement and develop in children an appreciation for classical music. It is our goal that every child participates, feels successful and, most importantly, thoroughly enjoys the music.

Our Goal

Fun with Composers brings classical music from what can seem to children like a complicated, mysterious form to one that is completely child-centered and fascinating. Musical concepts and skills are creatively woven into the lessons so the focus remains on imaginative fun.

All children should have the opportunity to experience classical music in a way that is meaningful and significant to them. With your help, we can take classical music from its seemingly elusive realm to one that is close to their hearts.

About the Author

Deborah Ziolkoski is an elementary music specialist with the Surrey School District in British Columbia. She has a bachelor of education with a music major, and her masters Orff level from the University of Memphis with Jos Wuytack. For the past two years, Deborah has designed the teacher-guided activities for the Vancouver Symphony Orchestra's elementary school concerts. In 2005, her Orff Club performed the Persian March and Aquarium (as written in *Fun with Composers*) with the Vancouver Symphony Orchestra.

Deborah has over fifteen years' experience as a music specialist. Her Orff groups have been asked to perform at many events including the National Orff Conference. Deborah lives in White Rock, British Columbia with her husband, Ed, and their three children, Annika, Lauren, and Charlize.

Fun with Composer
Teaching Tools Guarantee Success!

Reproducible Pages
Finally a guide that is truly teacher friendly! *Fun with Composers* encourages teachers to reproduce materials for classroom use and their students. Composer images, biographies, music maps and activity pages are designed to enrich children's learning experience.

CDs and DVDs
Our CDs have fun lyrics that encourage the children to sing along, and assist parents as they help their children follow the music maps. The children will also enjoy the orchestral arrangement which immediately follows.

On our DVD, the lessons taped were a condensed version of our Teacher's Guides instructed to non-auditioned students in one fifty-minute class. Real students in a real setting! The DVDs demonstrate the teaching process and the key teaching strategies, as well as the final outcomes of each piece.

As many of the orchestral pieces were not originally written for the voice, it was difficult to keep the pieces all within the proper register for a child. When you find sections that are too low, or high, I recommend these sections be spoken and used as rhythmic speech patterns rather than choral sections.

Music Maps
Our music maps provide a wonderful visual arrangement of the music. The purpose of the maps is to place the music in a structured, organized format so children have a better understanding of its sequence. Children of all ages benefit from the maps, for they help children "make sense" of the music. The music maps provide a visual reminder of all the movement, song, and dance they experienced in class.

Children are also thrilled when they can instantly take home these maps and share them with their parents. Teachers are highly encouraged to provide copies of the maps for the students for these purposes! I recommend making class sized maps by enlarging our version to an 11 x 17 size, and gluing onto colorful poster paper. The purchase of our Just for Kids Guides (CDs included) insures that children will be sharing, enjoying, and truly reaping the benefits of these unique, child-centered maps.

"Just for Kids" Guides
(CDs included)

Fun with Composer's Children's Guides are a "take-home" version of our Teacher Guides. Composer images and stories, music maps, activity pages, intriguing stories and a CD which brings these pages to life! Our CDs include two recordings of each selection. The first version will have lyrics sung over the music so children can easily sing along, and parents can help guide their children when conducting through the music maps.

The second version is an authentic orchestral recording. This gives children the opportunity to internalize the lyrics and appreciate the music as it was originally written. We encourage parents to play the CD whenever possible. Watch out Hilary Duff! The music of great classical composers such as Mozart, Grieg, and Strauss will be the new requested favourites!

When should the "Just for Kids" order forms be distributed?
We recommend the order forms be distributed *after a few selections have been introduced.* In this way, children will be excited about their music, and take pride in sharing it with friends and family.

Can children who have not been taught the lessons in the classroom benefit from the "Just for Kids" Guides?
We have included simple guided activities for parents so that they are able to help their child sing, dance, act and play through the classics. The guides include stories which will help children and parents alike understand the significance of the lyrics and the activities which correspond.

How to order the "Just for Kids" Guides
Order forms are enclosed in this copy, or materials may be ordered through our website or teachers.

Fun with Composers as a Classroom Fundraiser
15% of the classroom teacher's total sales of "Just for Kids" Guidebooks will be donated back to the classroom or music teacher. Teachers are responsible for the distribution and collection of all orders and monies. Cheques are to be made payable to Fun with Composers. Teachers may place orders by fax, mail, or through our website.

Coming Soon
A picture book series including "The Ringmaster and the Tightrope Walker," "The Snobby Pears," and more! Watch for our children's DVD, which will include singing and dancing to these wonderful stories. Perfect for children ages 3–6!

Special Thanks

...to Ruth Wiwchar for her endless support, assistance, and her belief in this project. Ruth's passion, expertise, and guidance in music have been invaluable.

...to my husband Ed who has been an amazing business partner and support throughout this entire project. Without your encouragement, love, support, patience and advice, this would not have been possible. Thank-you for believing in me!

...to my three children, Annika, Lauren, and Charlize who have inspired many of my ideas! I could not have asked for more wonderful children!

...to Bramwell and Lana Tovey, Stephanie Wallin, and the Vancouver Symphony Orchestra for all their support, encouragement, and desire to bring Classical music into the classrooms and homes of every child!

...to all of my wonderful school students who first shared and helped develop these classical creations over time. A special thank you to all my former Robert Browning students.

...to the Laronde Elementary staff, students, and parents who participated in the creation of the DVD. You were all great to work with. Thank you!

...to Joyce Boorman who first inspired me with her wonderful, creative lessons of Percy the Balloon and the Potato Dance.

...to my sister Karen who is a constant inspiration to me. Your creative talents, energy and passion have made you the exceptional teacher that you are today. Thank you for guiding me in the right direction, and sharing your love of music with me!

...to my dad who patiently sat through hour upon hour of piano lessons, and nurtured my love of music. You always believed in me, and helped me strive to be my very best.

...to my mom who always encouraged my projects, to my sister Cindy and my brother Rick who have always encouraged my entrepreneurial ventures.

...to Carolyn Boyes, Debra Yacheson, Cheri Peters, Bree Van Ness, Heather Provencher, Jodi Trudeau, Marceline Moody, Vic Hooper, Vic Mollot, Michelle Agar, Donna Beynon-Patterson, Daryl Reimer, and all the other amazing teachers and friends whom I have learned so much from and who have always been supportive and encouraging.

Last but not least, to my amazing team which helped put this book together: Eric Olson, Jim Fee, Heidi Groschler, Corena Akeson, Jeff Tymoschuk, Jim Littleford, Jason Fredricson, In-Vancouver Web Design, and Blaine Kyllo. Thank-you all!

Contents

Foreword

Fun with Composers brings the great classics to life! The power of storytelling will draw children into the intriguing world of classical music!

Secret agents, rattling skeletons, and dancing knights are just a few of the fascinating characters unveiled in this unique union of story and song. Children will sing, dance, act, and play to the music of Strauss, Mozart, and other greats!

Our flexible guides are geared to accommodate curricula for children aged 3-12, giving teachers the freedom to select from a wide range of themes, music, and composers. Music and concepts have been carefully selected to suit the developmental age and skill levels of the child.

Detailed lesson plans, reproducible pages, a CD (with lyrics sung over the music and the orchestral recording) as well as a DVD of these lessons being instructed make it possible for a teacher with little or no music background to teach the guide successfully. Absolutely foolproof!

Fun with Composers may be implemented in whole or in part, and may be adapted to reflect the teacher's own style. If a teacher chooses to utilize the guide fully, children can experience up to twenty-seven classical lessons over the course of the year.

Our guides are designed to enrich a curriculum and nurture the many ways in which children learn. The lessons are sequential, each beginning with an introduction to the composer. Stories, music, movement, and instrumental play are then woven into subsequent lessons. Although non-pitched percussion instruments enhance the child's learning experience, they are not essential to teach the lessons.

To reinforce and enrich the child's experience, *Fun with Composers* has developed "Just for Kids" guides (CDs included). Through the purchase of the "Just for Kids" guides, children will be encouraged to share their experiences and newfound interest in classical music with family and friends.

Music is an invaluable gift for all ages. Together, we can help children develop a greater understanding and appreciation for the great classics!

Sincerely,
Deborah Ziolkoski

Let's Warm Up!

Having children warm up with some basic loco-motor movements is a great way to begin any lesson. Single movements or combinations may be used depending on to what extent you would like to use movement in your teaching.

Basic loco-motor movement stimulus is introduced on the hand drum using a mallet. Begin with the simplest of movements, and with each stimulus presented, encourage the children's imagination and draw out their creative energy.

Here are a few suggestions:
- Use terms "super ears" and "super stomping feet" (to encourage them to listen intently and quickly respond to stimuli).
- Use stick figure drawings on cards to add variation to movement combinations. Ask children to freeze in these positions.

- Use phrases such as "walk like a giant", or "skip like a burly pirate." Encourage moving at different levels (high, medium, or low).
- Challenge children by having them move to a small, repetitive movement pattern a few times, and then signal them to stop. Have volunteers verbalize what combination of movements they were doing and then demonstrate them to the class. Write a few simple patterns notated on the board. Can they identify the pattern you just played?
- Ask children to work in small groups to create their own combinations of movements. Have them perform these for the class. Take this a step further and ask students to make up an accompaniment for their movement combinations on non-pitched percussion instruments.

Basic Loco-motor Movements   *Hand Drum Stimuli*

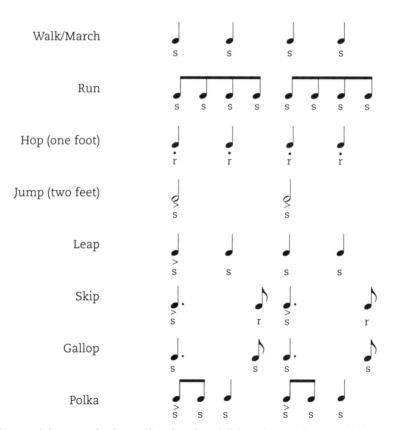

When playing, use a mallet for precision. On the hop stimulus, let children know that a quick tap on the skin indicates a change of feet.

s: indicates a tapping of the drum skin.

r: indicates the drum rim.

Recommended Instruments

Non-pitched percussion instruments are a wonderful way to enhance any musical experience. The following list of instruments provides a wide assortment that will provide the children with an opportunity to be creative in their play. Instruments may be purchased at most music stores or through mail order.

Rhythm sticks and/or claves (come in pairs)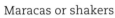

Maracas or shakers

Triangle

Jingle bells

Hand drum (I recommend two)

Sand blocks (come in pairs)

Tambourine

Cluster bells

Guiro

Finger cymbals (come in pairs)

Large Cymbal

Cabasa

Helpful Tips

*A top hat and a sparkly wand are great for conducting.
*Streamers or sheer scarves really enhance movement.
*Stick figure cards are a great way to add fun to movement activities! These are quick and easy to make.

When do I introduce the composers?
With each new composer studied, it is recommended that the first portion of each unit be used to introduce children to the composer.

Interesting stories of the composers' lives and simple images are provided to help children feel a real connection and have a better understanding of these intriguing composers.

Rondo Alla Turca
(Mystery of King Lou)
MUSIC: W.A. MOZART; MUSIC MAP: D. ZIOLKOSKI

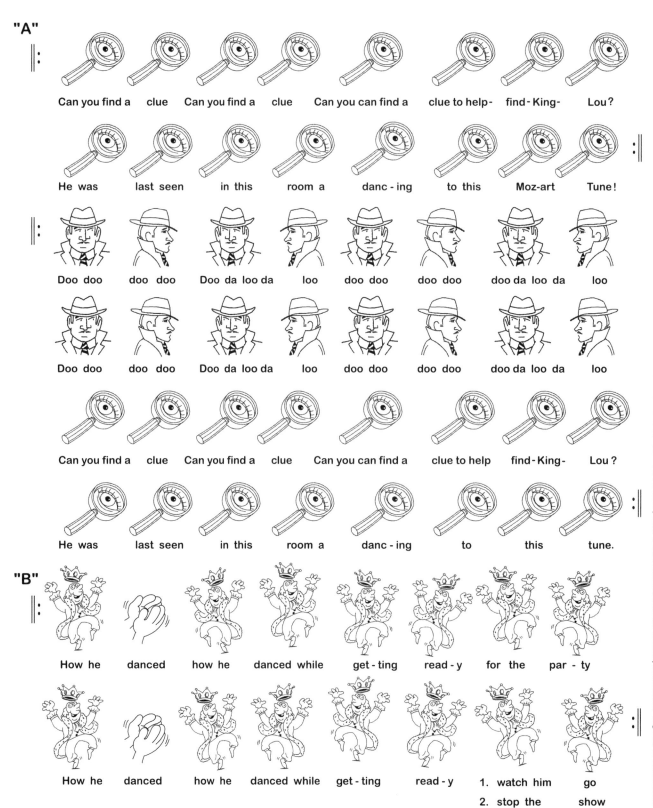

"C"

Dusting (32 beats)

Scrubbing ‖: (16 beats)

Dusting (16 beats) :‖

Return to section:

"B"   "A'"   "B"

CODA ‖:

Where's the | King ——— gone ——— | look | look | look | Hmm?

where oh | where | could | — he | King ——— | Lou ———

Look | Look | Look ——— Hmm? | Lou's ——— | real ly | real ly | gone

So long | Good - bye — farewell — | we | hope | to see you | soon | ———

KING   LOU

Final form A B C B A B   Coda

Rondo Alla Turca

(Mystery of King Lou)

MUSIC: W.A. MOZART; LYRICS D. ZIOLKOSKI

A Can you find a clue can you find a clue... Can you find a clue to help find King__ Lou? He was...

B How he danced how he danced while get-ting rea-dy for the par-ty how he...

C Maids dusting

Butlers scrubbing

Final form: A B C B A B Coda

Due to the length of this selection, only the first five measures have been provided.

Orff Orchestration

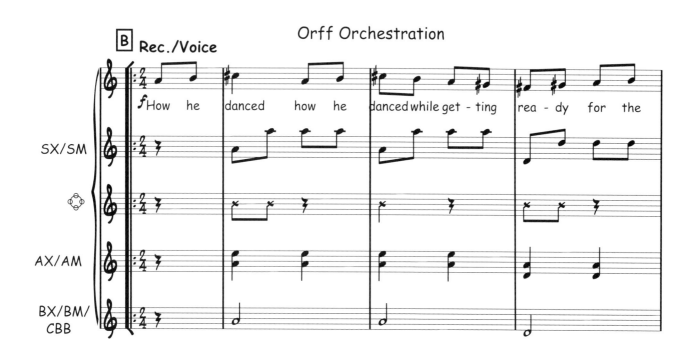

Rondo Alla Turca

(Mystery of King Lou)

MUSIC: W.A. MOZART

Goal
To familiarize students with "Rondo Alla Turca" by Mozart. Students will be able to recognize, sing, play, and move to each section of the rondo.

Related Concepts
Understand and distinguish between piano and forté and the term rondo.

Recommended Grade: grade 3+

Suggested Themes
Mysteries

Formation
Scattered position, seated on the floor.

The Mystery of King Lou

Many years ago, there was a very fun king named King Lou. He wasn't your ordinary type of king, for all he liked to do was hold great parties and dance.

From morning to night, this king would dance down the royal halls of his palace practicing the latest dance steps while listening to the music of his favourite composer, Wolfgang Amadeus Mozart.

The only other thing that he would think about other than his dance steps were what new clothes he should wear and what type of decorations he should put up for his next party. He never gave any thought to other important matters that concerned most kings.

Although the people of his kingdom thought King Lou was an amusing leader and a great party host, they were worried that their kingdom would fall apart if he continued to rule the land.

Many people believed there needed to be more rules in place because the kingdom was beginning to get a little crazy! Some people even thought that King Lou should be expelled from the kingdom and replaced by a new king!

One night, right before a great royal gala, the king disappeared. No one seemed to know where he went. It was almost as if he had disappeared into thin air!

Where could King Lou have gone? Some people thought he danced his way down one of the many long royal halls, got lost in the maze, and couldn't find his way back. Others thought the maids and butlers had locked him up in one of the thousands of little rooms in the palace so they wouldn't have to watch him singing and dancing anymore.

Or, perhaps some of the people from his kingdom who were secretly wishing for a new king had carried him out during the night and thrown him aboard a pirate ship!

No one really knows for sure, but if you hear a voice singing and feet tapping in the middle of the night, you know that King Lou might be near by. Would you like to learn his favourite song and dance in case he shows up at your door? Nothing would be more fun than singing and dancing with King Lou!

Lesson One

Objective
To teach Section A. Children will sing, dance, and move to Section A.

Suggested Teaching Process
Teach Section A

- Read students the story, "The Mystery of King Lou."
- Ask students if they would like to learn King Lou's famous song and dance. *(A quick glance of the Summary of Suggested Movements located at the end of Lesson Three will provide an overview of the actions for the entire piece.)*
- Invite the students onto the floor and have them listen as you play the hand drum to a marching cue. Ask what type of movement they think fits this sound best. (Marching.)
- Can the students move around like a detective searching for clues to that marching sound? (Needs to be fairly fast to fit the music's tempo.)

- Ask students to listen as you play eight beats on the hand drum with a quick sixteenth-note tap before the final eighth beat. Did they recognize the change? Tell students that when they hear the quick tap (or an accented eighth beat) to quickly find a partner. Do this a few times so students recognize the phrase length.
- Demonstrate the body percussion section, pretending to have a partner in front of you: *patsch, patsch, patsch, patsch,* clap own hands twice, clap partner's hands twice, clap own hands once. *(refer to Suggested Actions/Movements at the end of this unit)*
- Ask the students to try this pattern with you, pretending to be your partner. When the students are comfortable with this pattern, ask them to try it with a partner.
- Put the two sections together. Have the students listen as you play eight beats on the hand drum and then perform body percussion immediately after on the next eight beats. Can they join you? Invite students to march around on the floor, finding a new partner by the eighth beat. They will then perform the new body percussion pattern with their partner. Practice this a few times until the students are secure with it.
- After the students can perform these two sections together, ask them to listen as you introduce Section A through rhythmic speech: "Can you find a clue? Can you find a clue? Can you find a clue to help find King Lou? He was last seen in this room a-dancing to this Mozart tune." Have the students echo this back to you a few times until they are secure with it. Use different, fun voices to make it interesting!
- Say it aloud with the students, this time adding in the hand drum on the first eight beats, and body percussion on the second eight. Ask the students to join you on the floor, moving to the drum with you.
- Try this a few times, asking the students to try to find a new partner at the end of each hand drum pattern (on the word "Lou").
- When the students seem comfortable performing the speech and movement pattern together, teach them the melody by having them echo it back to you phrase by phrase.

- The middle section (Doo, doo, doo, doo…) is a series of upward and downward patterns where the students can pretend to look for clues. Play this section using the recording with the lyrics.
- Encourage the students to switch directions at the end of each phrase. I find that by simply demonstrating, they quickly follow. Sing along on the syllable "doo" (or whichever combinations of "doo" sounds come naturally, i.e. doo doo doo doo doo da loo da loo).
- This section will then end with the same two phrases found at the beginning of the music. Review it from the beginning, singing and dancing through the music of Section A.
- Ask the students to listen and think about how they are supposed to be moving to the music, as you play the first track of "Rondo Alla Turca" for them. (Play up to the end of Section A only.) Try singing and dancing with the CD. First try the recording with the lyrics, then with the instrumental version. Stop at the end of Section A.

Lesson Two

Objective
Introduce students to sections B and C, singing, dancing, and acting through these sections. Identify the difference in dynamics between the sections. Introduce the terms forté and piano.

Suggested Props
Colourful feathers to be used as "dusters" and sponges to be used as "scrubbers" for the maids and butlers.

Suggested Teaching Process
Review Section A, singing, dancing, and acting through the music with the CD.

Section B
Option #1

Place your hands on your hips and move forward then backwards 2x. (SEE FIGURE #1)

Option #2: Royal Dance

Place your hands on your hips on the words "how he," and then on the first "danced" clap 2x. Move forward doing step-step-step-hop, feet together, and then repeat the same steps moving backwards returning to the original spot. (SEE FIGURE #2)

Option #3: Improvisation

- Introduce Section B by explaining to the students that this is where King Lou really got to show off his dancing skills! How would a king dance? Discuss the possibilities with the students, asking for volunteers to demonstrate if possible.
- Teach the students the melody for Section B.
- When the students are secure with the melody, ask them to create their own King Lou dance. Students can try this on their own, in partners, or in small groups. Students will develop a good feeling of phrase length through this exercise.

The music lends itself to a marching/stepping movement with perhaps some interesting arm movements, turns, and exploration of space (moving high, medium, or low). Encourage the students to move creatively by asking them if they can move their arms, heads, torso, etc., in a fun way.

*Ask various students to demonstrate for the class, even asking half the class to watch while the other dances, and then switch.

In the suggested actions, movement has been choreographed for those teachers who may not feel comfortable with this improvisation segment. Feel free to use to your discretion.

- When the students feel at ease with Section B, review it from the top with the assistance of the CD. Proceed with Section C.

Section C:

Improvisation: Maids and butlers dusting/scrubbing

Sequence:

Maids dusting: "Piano"

- Identified as the first thirty-two beats; a series of "busy" sixteenth-note runs played piano (softly).

Butlers scrubbing: "Forté"

- Identified as the following sixteen beats played "forté" (loudly).

Maids dusting: "Piano"

- Sixteen beats played piano.

Repeat the final two butlers scrubbing and maids dusting sequence, this time using thirty-two beats for each part.

Play Section C (instrumental version) for the students, asking them to relax and listen.

FIGURE #1

forward	How he	danced,	how he	danced	while	get-ting	read-y	for the	part-y
		step	step	step		hop	step	step	step
backward	How he	danced,	how he	danced	while	get-ting	read-y	watch him	go
	hop	step	step	step		hop	step	step	step together
forward	How he	danced,	how he	danced	while	get-ting	read-y	for the	part-y
		step	step	step		hop	step	step	step
backward	How he	danced,	how he	danced	while	get-ting	read-y	stop the	show
	hop	step	step	step		hop	step	step	step together

FIGURE #2

forward	How he	danced,	how he	danced	while	get-ting	read-y	for the	part-y
		clap, clap		step		step	step	hop	step together
backward	How he	danced,	how he	danced	while	get-ting	read-y	watch him	go
		clap, clap		step		step	step	hop	step together
forward	How he	danced,	how he	danced	while	get-ting	read-y	for the	part-y
		clap, clap		step		step	step	hop	step together
backward	How he	danced,	how he	danced	while	get-ting	read-y	stop the	show
		clap, clap		step		step	step	hop	step together

- Explain to the students that this section was the "cleaning" music: The king's maids and butlers would get together to do a quick clean up to get rid of all the dust and dirt in the palace.
- Tell the students you came across the maids' and butlers' cleaning tools but you are not sure what they could be used for. Ask the students to brainstorm with you what they could be used for. (Guide the answers towards dusting and scrubbing.)
- Ask the students how they might be used. Place sponges and feathers on the floor and have the students create their own cleaning techniques as you play Section C of the music.
- After playing through Section C with the students improvising and exploring how they might use these sponges and feathers, stop the music and discuss which segments of the music best fit the feathers and which best fit the sponges. Why?

Possibly because feathers are lighter, they might suit the first thirty-two beats where the music is light, soft (piano), busy, and more of an uneven note patterning. Since sponges are a bit heavier, they can be used for a smooth downward and upward swipe of the hand, following the music. Feel free to adapt this sequence to your students' rationale: if it makes sense to them to do it some other way, let them create and enjoy.

- Which parts of Section C were soft and which were loud? (Maids dusting introduction was soft, followed by the louder butlers scrubbing music.) Use this time to reinforce the dynamic terms piano (soft) and forté (loud).
- Divide the students randomly into two groups: maids and butlers. Ask the maids to freeze in position when they hear the butler music commencing and vice versa. Switch parts, so that all the students have experienced being both a maid and a butler.
- Ask the students to decide whether they would like to be maids or butlers, distributing to them the appropriate cleaning tools. Tell them that they must keep the feathers and sponges tucked away somewhere until it is time for their part. Remind them that they must freeze when it is not their part.
- Review through Section C with the CD, and then teach the Coda. (*They will learn this special ending quickly just by listening to the lyrics sung on the cd.*) Explain to the students that a Coda is a special

ending.
- Review from the very beginning, using the CD first with the lyrics, and then the instrumental accompaniment.

Suggested Actions for Coda:
(shrug shoulders)
   "Where's the King gone?"

(searching in different directions on accented notes, shrugging shoulders on question mark)
   "look, look-look?"

(shrug shoulders)
   "Where, oh where, could he be?"

(hands on hips, looking frustrated)
   "King Lou…!"

(searching different directions on accents, and shrugging shoulders on question mark)
   "look, look-look?"

(hands on hips on "Lou's," nod head on "real," "real," "gone")
   "Lou's real-ly, real-ly gone!"

Coda repeats, the second time played with "piano" dynamic.

Last phrases played with "forté" dynamic.
(wave royal waves, first right, then left)
   "So long! Good-bye! Fare-well"

(hands clasped together in front of chest) (hands on hips)
   "We hope to see you soon, King Lou!"

Final Form: A B C B A B Coda

Lesson Three

This lesson is designed for teachers who have non-pitched percussion and barred Orff instruments at their disposal. It is to be used as an enrichment piece. If you do not have instruments of any sort, please refer to the final performance section at the end of this lesson, and omit the instrumental recommendations.

Objective

To learn a simple accompaniment on barred instruments for Section B and non-pitched percussion accompaniment for Section C.

Materials required

Barred instruments (xylophones, metallophones, etc.)

Suggested Teaching Process

The Orff orchestration for barred instruments may be adapted to suit the level of your students. Below you will find a few adaptations of the arrangement:

Section B

(Instrumental accompaniment optional)

Grade 3: Broken C bordun played on the heartbeat, with/without the special ending. (On the second last measure, play F, G, and high C as the final note.)

Grade 3–4: As written in the orchestration. If the orchestration is slightly too difficult, simplify it by playing the I, IV, V solid borduns or bass line played on beat one, followed by a quarter rest.

Grade 4+: As written in the orchestration.

Suggested Instrumentation: Section C

The non-pitched percussion instruments for Section C are to be played to the rhythm of the music. Experiment with the students to discover which sounds they prefer as the accompaniment.

1. Maracas or nails scratching a hand drum: quick, light, "dusting" sounds.

2. Sand blocks/guiro: butler's "scrubbing" sounds.

Suggested Teaching Process
General Guidelines: Section B Orff Orchestration

Due to the fast tempo of this selection on the CD, I recommend that this be learned and played as an enrichment piece rather than to accompany the CD.

- Begin by *patching* the heartbeat on your legs, having the students mirror you.
- Review the term bordun, explaining to the students that it is the first and the fifth notes of a particular scale. For example, the C bordun has the notes C and G (I and V). The F bordun has F and high C, and the G bordun has G and D.

An easy trick is to tell students that it is a "telephone" bordun. You always use the first and the fifth notes, and take away the three in the middle. When you do this, it looks like a pretend telephone!

Depending on the accompaniment you choose:

- Starting with the contra bass line (or the lowest part available). Mirror the pattern on your legs (as if the instrument were facing the students). For example: the low C would be on your right leg, the G your left. When students are secure with the pattern, sing it through while playing on your legs.
- Transfer from your body to the instrument. Hold the instrument upside down, so it appears positioned the correct way for the students. Demonstrate the part on the instrument. Have them sing along while mirroring on their legs.
- When one part is secure, ask the students to place that section in their memory banks and continue on to review the next parts. Always start teaching the lowest-ranged instrumental parts (contrabass bars, bass xylophones, metalophones, etc.) and work your way up to the highest- ranged instruments (glockenspiels, if available).
- When you have mirrored all the parts, I often will spend one entire class with just one or two instruments from each part placed in front of where the students are sitting. (C.B.B, BX , BM, AX, AM etc.)

May I suggest putting all the parts together in a small grouping such as this before moving over to a larger grouping of instruments. In this way, most students will have had an opportunity to come up and play, giving them both confidence and practice. It also provides the teacher with an opportunity to spot difficulties and help students in need.

Be careful not to overwhelm the students, as this will defeat the purpose. Take things slow and easy, starting with a simple C solid bordun played either to the heartbeat (every beat) or the pulse (the strong beat; in this case, every first beat) of the music. A bordun line with the addition of a tambourine or drum is a great accompaniment for young children!

Final Performance
Non-pitched percussion instruments:
*A small group of students can be positioned just off to the side of the movement area, ready to accompany Section C, each time it occurs.

Singers/Actors/Dancers:
*The remaining students will be responsible for singing and moving through the entire section. They must decide beforehand whether they will be maids or butlers, as they will need to tuck away their

sponge or feather for Section C. Remind the students that they are to freeze in Section C when it is not their part.

*If you have plenty of students, you may wish to divide students into three groups:
1. Non-pitched percussion players (will be responsible for accompanying the maids and butlers as they dust and scrub in Section C).
2. Detectives (will be responsible for sections A and B).
3. Maids and butlers (only move to their designated parts in Section C).

When the music returns to Section A, the maids and butlers can freeze like statues in a cleaning position, as the detectives resume their role. The maids and butlers then return to the floor when the Coda plays. Everyone sings/acts the Coda.

Summary of Suggested Movement/Actions

Section A: Secret agents
(March around the room searching for clues. Find a partner by the last beat of the phrase.)
Can you find a **clue**? **Can** you find a **clue**? **Can** you find a **clue** to hel-p fin-d King- Lou?

He was	last	seen	in	this	room	a-danc-ing	to this Moz-art	tune
	patsch	patsch	patsch	patsch	clap own	clap own	clap partners 2x	clapown

(Eight beat march, searching the room. Find a new partner on the word "Lou.")
Can you find a **clue**? **Can** you find a **clue**? **Can** you find a **clue** to hel-p fin-d King- Lou?

He was	last	seen	in	this	room	a-danc-ing	to this Moz-art	tune
	patsch	patsch	patsch	patsch	clap own	clap own	clap partners 2x	clapown

(Pretend to use magnifying glasses, searching in a different direction for each phrase [on bold "doos"], pausing on the last note "loo.")

Doo doo	doo doo	**doo**-da-loo-da-loo	**Doo** doo	doo doo	**doo**-da-loo-*da*-loo
Doo doo	doo doo	**doo**-da-loo-da-loo	**Doo** doo	doo doo	**doo**-da-loo-*da*-loo

(March around the room searching for clues. Find a partner by the last beat of the phrase.)
Can you find a **clue**? **Can** you find a **clue**? **Can** you find a **clue** to hel-p fin-d King- Lou?

He was	last	seen	in	this	room	a-danc-ing	to this Moz-art	tune
	patsch	patsch	patsch	patsch	clap own	clap own	clap partners 2x	clapown

Section B

Place your hands on your hips on the words "how he," and then on the first "danced" clap 2x. Move forward doing step-step-step-hop, feet together, and then repeat the same steps moving backwards returning to the original spot.

forward	How he	danced, clap, clap	how he	danced step	while	get-ting step	read-y step	for the hop	part-y step tog
backward	How he	danced, clap, clap	how he	danced step	while	get-ting step	read-y step	watch him hop	go step tog
forward	How he	danced, clap, clap	how he	danced step	while	get-ting step	read-y step	for the hop	part-y step tog
backward	How he	danced, clap, clap	how he	danced step	while	get-ting step	read-y step	stop the hop	show step tog

Section C: Maids and butlers cleaning improvisation

Dusting improvisation: Thirty-two beats. Maids dust using feathers as props and freeze in a dusting position when butlers' music starts.

Scrubbing/washing improvisation: Sixteen beats: Butlers scrub using sponges and freeze in a scrubbing position when maids' music starts.

Dusting improvisation: Sixteen beats.

Scrubbing and dusting: Repeat (thirty-two beats each).

Section B – Royal Dance
Section A – Secret agents
Section B – Royal Dance

Coda

(shrug shoulders)
"Where's the King gone?"

(Searching in different directions on accented notes.)
"Look, look-look"

(shrug shoulders)
"Where, oh where, could he be?"

(Hands on hips.)
"King Lou…"

(Look different directions on accents.)
"Look, look, look?"

(Hands on hips on "Lou's," nod head on "real," "real," "gone")
"Lou's real-ly, real-ly gone!"

Repeat with "piano" dynamic.

Final phrase: forté (wave and blow kisses)
"So long! Good-bye! Fare-well"
"We hope to see you soon, King Lou!"

Final Form: A B C B A B Coda

Tritsch Tratsch Polka

(The Ringmaster and the Tightrope Walker)

MUSIC: J. STRAUSS II; MUSIC MAP: D. ZIOLKOSKI

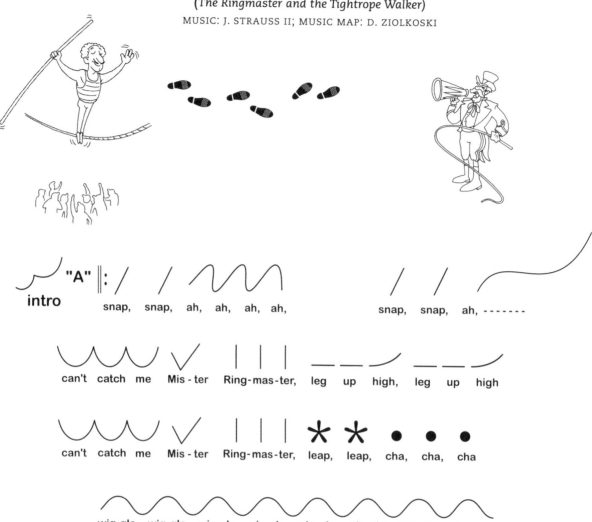

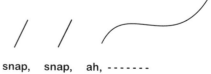

intro "A"

snap, snap, ah, ah, ah, ah,   snap, snap, ah, - - - - - -   2X

can't catch me Mis-ter Ring-mas-ter, leg up high, leg up high

can't catch me Mis-ter Ring-mas-ter, leap, leap, cha, cha, cha

wig-gle, wig-gle, wig-gle, wig-gle, wig-gle, wig-gle, wig-gle, wig-gle,

falling, falling, falling, falling, I am falling down

I can do it, I can do it, I can do it, I can do it,

do it, do it, do it, do it, do it, do it, do it, do it,

snap, snap, ah, ah, ah, ah,   snap, snap, ah, - - - - - -   2X

26

Intermission:

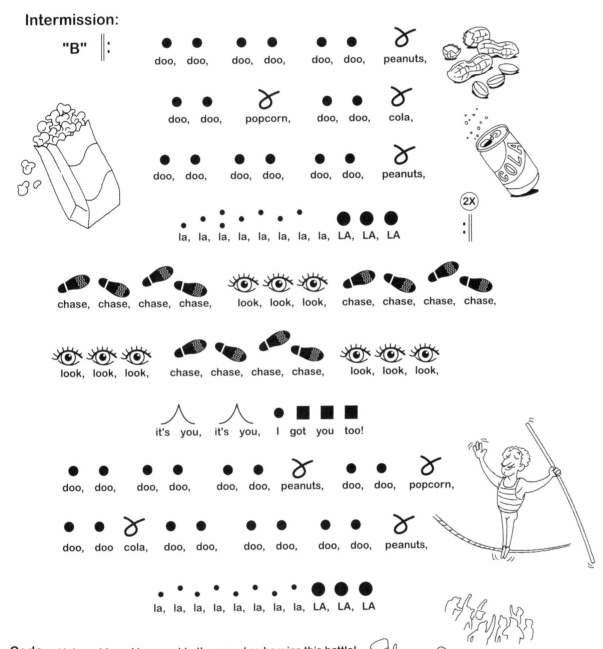

"B"

doo, doo, doo, doo, doo, doo, peanuts,

doo, doo, popcorn, doo, doo, cola,

doo, doo, doo, doo, doo, doo, peanuts,

2X

la, la, la, la, la, la, la, la, LA, LA, LA

chase, chase, chase, chase, look, look, look, chase, chase, chase, chase,

look, look, look, chase, chase, chase, chase, look, look, look,

it's you, it's you, I got you too!

doo, doo, doo, doo, doo, doo, peanuts, doo, doo, popcorn,

doo, doo cola, doo, doo, doo, doo, doo, doo, peanuts,

la, la, la, la, la, la, la, la, LA, LA, LA

Coda (Johnny blows kisses out to the crowd as he wins this battle! The Ringmaster is fuming mad!)

Final Form: A B A Coda

27

Tritsch Tratsch Polka

(The Ringmaster and the Tightrope Walker)

MUSIC: J. STRAUSS II; ARR./LYRICS: D. ZIOLKOSKI

Introduction

28

snap   snap   Ah Ah Ah Ah   snap Ah snap Ah Ah Ah Ah

B Trio

Doo   Doo   Doo Doo   Doo Doo   (Pea - nuts)   Doo Doo   (Pop - corn)

Doo Doo   (Co - la)   Doo Doo   Doo Doo   Doo Doo   (Pea - nuts)

spoken:

la, la, la, la,   la, la, la, la,   la,   la,   la.   (Its Chase chase chase chase look - look

look, its   Chase chase chase chase   look   look   look   its   chase chase chase chase

look   look   look its you   its you   I   got you   too!) Doo doo   doo doo   doo doo

(Pea - nuts!) Doo doo   (Pop - corn) Doo doo   (Co - la) Doo doo

D.S. al CODA

doo   doo   doo doo   (Pea - nuts) la, la, la, la   la, la, la, la,   la,   la   la

CODA

(Johnny blows kisses   to   audience   and   wave   as

ring   master   fumes!)

Final form: A B A

29

Tritsch Tratsch Polka

(The Ringmaster and the Tightrope Walker)

MUSIC: JOHANN STRAUSS

Goal

To familiarize students with "Tritsch Tratsch Polka" by Johann Strauss. Students will be able to sing, dance and play through the music and conduct through the music map successfully.

Related Concepts

A B A (ternary) form.

Recommended Grade

Preschool–grade 6 (adapt instrumental accompaniment accordingly).

Suggested Themes

Circus

Formation

Students are in a scattered formation for the duration of the story. When putting Section A together, strings may be taped to the floor acting as tightropes. Ringmasters are at one end of the rope and the tightrope walkers around the middle. Section B will have students moving freely about the room.

Materials required

String/yarn taped on floor for tightropes. (Ten to twelve ropes or lines of masking tape will do) CD, class-sized music map, picture books.

Lesson One

Objectives

Read story (lesson strategies for Section A incorporated within). Teach Section A (as per story).

Suggested Teaching Process

A great way to introduce the concept of a circus is to begin a discussion with the aid of a few picture books. There are many to choose from!

The Ringmaster and the Tightrope Walker

Section A

Many years ago, there was a mean, selfish ringmaster. He always wanted to be the main attraction at every circus. He made certain that other circus performers had very little time in the spotlight, for he wanted all the attention! He believed that it was his show, and that he should be the star!

During every circus act, the ringmaster would crack his whip to show everyone that he was the most powerful and the best. One day the circus needed to hire a new tightrope walker for their show. They hired a talented young boy who seemed to be very good at his act. In fact, the ringmaster thought he was a little too good!

So he decided to try and scare the tightrope walker off his rope. He had a scowl on his face, and with a sharp snap of his wrist his whip cracked loudly through the air—not once, but twice.

(Refer to the music for the rhythmic notation of the lyrics)
Teacher asks students to demonstrate while saying, "Snap, snap."

Well, with two loud cracks like that, the tightrope walker became very nervous and cried out, "Ah, ah, ah, ah!" as he stumbled around on his rope!

Ask students to demonstrate what a scared tightrope walker crying out, "Ah, ah, ah, ah!" might look like.

Realizing that this was a very talented tightrope walker, the ringmaster continued to crack his whip until he realized his plan was not working!

(Repeat snapping whip and "Ah, ah, ah,ah" part four times.)

To make things worse, the tightrope walker looked at him with a big smile on his face and in a teasing manner sang, "Can't catch me Mis-ter Ring-mas-ter, leg up high, leg up high; can't catch me Mis-ter Ring-mas-ter, leap, leap, cha, cha, cha."

Teacher demonstrates how the ringmaster was getting teased while singing the section above. Ask all students to try.

This made the ringmaster so furious, that he bent down and began wiggling the rope trying to get him off.

Teacher demonstrates saying: "Wig-gle, wig-gle, wig-gle, wig-gle, wig-gle, wig-gle, wig-gle, wig-gle."

This trick almost worked, for the tightrope walker shouted out, "Fal-ling, fal-ling, fal-ling, fal-ling, I am fal-ling down!" *(Teacher's voice falls from high to low.)*

Just as the ringmaster thought he had won, the tightrope walker caught his balance at the bottom of the rope.

Teacher asks students how they might fall down if the ringmaster were wiggling the rope. (Ask students what clues from your voice were heard – high to low.) Rehearse from the beginning point of wiggling the rope.

The tightrope walker refused to let the ringmaster get the best of him and began saying, "I can do it, I can do it, I can do it, I can do it, do it, do it, do it…"

*Have students act this out along with the teacher, as the teacher repeats words, "I can do it…" (rising from a low balancing position to a high one).

So, with the ringmaster cracking his whip, the tightrope walker began gaining back his balance. The battle began once again with "snap, snap…"

Teacher points to herself/himself and says "snap, snap," then points to students. They should say, "Ah, ah, ah, ah!" (Repeat this four times alternating "ahs" as in the music.)

- Ask students if they would like to become ringmasters and tightrope walkers?
- Divide students into two groups: ringmasters and tightrope walkers. Ask the ringmasters to find their places at the ends of the ropes (one ringmaster per rope, two if necessary). Tightrope walkers are to find a spot in the middle of the ropes. Ideally, there should be one student per rope, but there can be two, if necessary.
- You may also have a section of students who are on the sidelines watching and singing. Switch turns allowing these students to participate after reviewing through it once.
- After the students have all had a chance to sing,

dance, and act out both the ringmaster and the tightrope walker parts for Section A, ask them to take a seat on the floor in front of you.

- Tell the students you were at the circus that had this mean ringmaster, and you managed to get a copy of the music that he had there. Explain to the students that the ringmaster's favourite music was by composer Johann Strauss. Do they remember anything special about Mr. Strauss? (Discuss a few highlights.)
- Explain to the students that this special piece is called "Tritsch Tratsch Polka." Can they say such a funny name? It really means "Chit Chat Polka."
- Ask students to listen carefully, to see if they can hear the ringmaster and tightrope walker's magic words. Play Section A, quietly whispering or singing along. (This often leads into doing the actions on the spot as well.)
- Would they like to try to be the ringmasters and tightrope walkers to the real music? Ask students to find a spot on the ropes, and sing, dance, and act through with the CD.

*I find it works best if you ask students to pick their own parts. Place all the ringmasters at the ends of the ropes (remind children that these ringmasters have no idea how to tightrope walk) and place tightrope walkers in the middles of the ropes. Remind tightrope walkers to place their arms out to keep their balance.

If time permits, you may like to introduce the music map at the end of this lesson. If not, take fifteen minutes another time and work through the music map then. Proceed as follows:

Introduce Section A of the music map
- Ask students to take a seat on the floor in front of the music map.
- Have students take out their conducting fingers, and ask them to conduct in the air as you conduct through Section A of the map.
- Students can sing along with you as together you conduct through the map. Demonstrate how the map works the first time just by singing. The second time, sing it through with the CD.
- When students are really secure with how the map works, ask volunteers to come up and conduct for the class.

*Don't forget a special conducting hat and wand for fun!

Lesson Two

Objectives
Introduce Section B, singing and dancing through the entire section. Review the entire piece in its full form (A B A). Introduce Section B of the music map, and have students conduct through both sections.

Suggested Teaching Process
Review through Section A, and when students are secure continue on with Section B.

Section B
(Refer to the music for the rhythmic notation of the lyrics)

- Ask students what other people they might see at the circus besides the performers. (People who sell peanuts and popcorn {vendors}.)

- Explain how, very often in circuses, there is an intermission or a short break between acts. During this break, vendors try to sell their treats. The vendors in this circus, however, each want to sell more treats than the others. They all walk around as though they have the best treats in the land.

- Ask students what types of treats there might be, drawing out answers like, peanuts, popcorn, and cola from students. Ask students to demonstrate how these vendors walk around calling out, "Peanuts, popcorn, cola!" Join the students, demonstrating Section B.

- Sing and act through Section B together. "Doo, doo, doo, doo, doo, doo, peanuts! Doo, doo, popcorn! Etc." Shout out the treat words in a way that a vendor might.

  Tell children the vendors "show off" at the end of the phrase by singing: "La, la, la, la, la, la, la, la, La, La, La" in a teasing way.
- Explain to students that the vendors all thought that everything was going really well, until a thief grabbed a treat from their treat box. Then the chase began!

Teacher demonstrates the chase taking swift, giant steps on the word chase, (strongly emphasize that there are only

four chase steps). Students freeze in a searching pose on the words "look, look, look."

"Chase, chase, chase, chase, look, look, look. Chase, chase, chase, chase, look, look, look. Chase, chase, chase, chase, look, look, look.

It's you, it's you, I got you too! *(Pretends to find thief and points at them.)*

Ask students to try this with you. Practice from the start of Section B.

After the vendor caught the thief, he didn't want anyone to think anything was wrong, so he continued on just like he did before. (Sing and move to the last line of Section B).

Ask students if they can stand up and act like one of the vendors at the circus. Sing, dance, and act this part through together.

Introduce Section B of the music map:
Ask students to take a seat on the floor by the large class music map. Have students conduct through Section B in the air, as you conduct on the class-sized map. Have a few volunteers come and guest conduct, with you remaining close by to help guide.

If time permits, practice through the entire song with the recording, having designated ringmasters and tightrope walkers for Section A (on designated ropes).

Tell students that after Section A, everyone magically transformed into vendors for Section B (scattered formation). Students then return to their original positions when the music returns to Section A.

Lesson Three

Objectives

Review through "Tritsch Tratsch Polka" in its entirety (A B A).

Add in instrumental accompaniment (optional).

Suggested Teaching Process

- Review through the entire selection, listening to the CD while conducting through a large class music map.
- As a class, try to find instruments to best fit the music. Below are *suggested instrumental accompaniments*, which you may like to try.

Suggested Instrumentation: Section A

(Play to the rhythm of the lyrics. Refer to the music for the rhythmic notation)

1. Tambourine or whip: Ringmaster's whip snapping "snap, snap."

2. Vibra slap or maracas: "Ah, ah, ah, ah!" of tightrope walker.

3. Cabassa: "Can't get me Mr. Ringmaster, leap, leap, cha, cha, cha!"

4. Guiro: "Wig-gle, wig-gle, wig-gle, wig-gle…"

5. Temple blocks or rhythm sticks: "Fal-ling, fal-ling, fal-ling, fal-ling…."

6. Hand drum or cymbal: "down"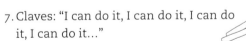

7. Claves: "I can do it, I can do it, I can do it, I can do it…"

Section B

1. Jingle bells: "Doo, doo, doo,doo, doo, doo."

2. Cow bell or triangle: "Peanuts, popcorn, cola."

3. Maracas: "La la la la la la la la La La La!"

4. Drum: "Chase, chase, chase, chase,"

5. Triangle or agogo bells: "look, look, look."

- Ask half of the students to accompany along on the instruments, as the others perform the movement. Ask one student to act as the guest conductor. Switch parts.
- Ask students if they know what the order of the piece was? (A B A)

Final Performance

If performing for another group of children or parents, the teacher can read the story to the audience, which would be followed by the students singing, dancing, and acting to the music. Half the students could be singing, dancing, and acting, with the other half accompanying on the recommended instruments.

Symphony no. 40
MUSIC: W.A. MOZART; MUSIC MAP: D. ZIOLKOSKI

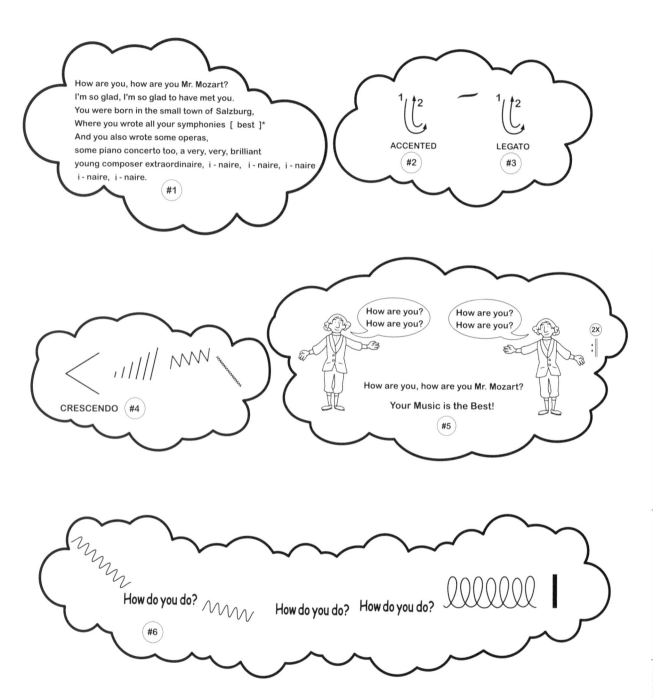

Symphony no. 40

MUSIC: W.A. MOZART; LYRICS: LEANNA LOEWEN; ARR: D. ZIOLKOSKI

Bubble #1

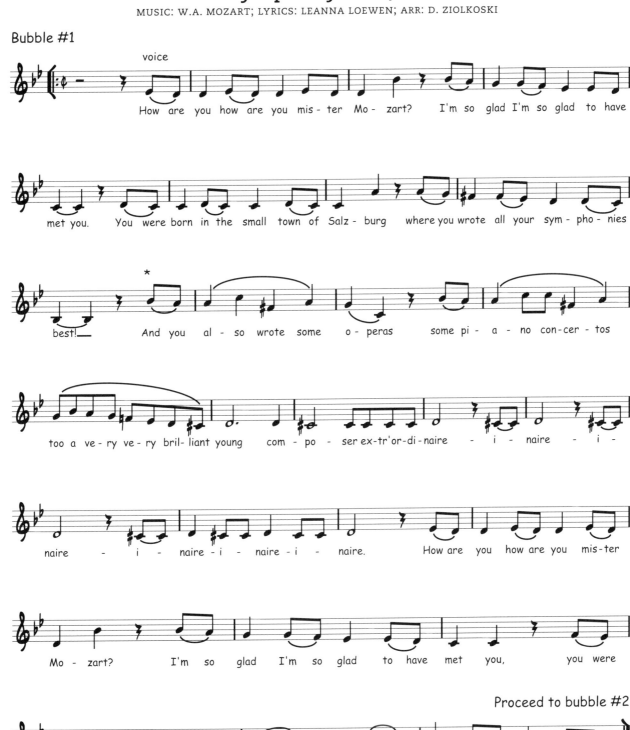

* On the second repeat, proceed to conducting pattern for bubble number 2.

Symphony no. 40

MUSIC: W.A. MOZART

Lesson One

Goal

To familiarize students with the opening section of "Symphony no. 40." Students will recognize/accompany specific sections with non-pitched percussion instruments. (Time allotted will vary, depending on students' levels.)

Related Concepts

Recognition of the theme and specific sections, 2/2 conducting pattern, accents, legato, crescendo, forté and piano dynamics, the terms ascending, descending.

Recommended Grade: grade 2+

Suggested Themes

Composers

Materials Required

Music map, Non-pitched percussion instruments, CD.

May I suggest that you take the time to review, and become secure with, the listening map before presenting it to the students. It may take you a few times of following the numbers on the bubbles before you are secure. Refer to the DVD for visual assistance. Although recommended, instruments are not essential.

Bubbles 1 to 5

Objective

To sing and conduct through bubbles 1 to 6 on the music map.

Suggested Teaching Process

- **Bubble #1**: Sing through the lyrics of the first bubble in its entirety. Create simple actions for these lyrics together as a class.
- Teach the phrases either by rote or with the assistance of words written on a class-sized music map. (Make a classroom-sized version if possible.) Which part must they repeat before going onto the next bubble? (The first four phrases, up to the word "best.")
- When the students are secure with this, play them the CD recording. Ask them to listen to the lyrics sung on the recording. Stop the recording at the end of bubble #1 and have them sing through with you as you play that section on the CD a second time.

Let's Conduct!

Bubbles #2 and **#3** are for conductors. Ask the students to conduct along with you. Demonstrate the pattern to conduct duple time. *(Make a backwards "J". Refer to the music map. Remember to do this backwards since the students will be mirroring you.)*

- Show students how to conduct if the music is accented or sharp sounding. How would one conduct if the music were legato/smooth? Help the students conduct the legato portion by having them pretend to conduct with a penny (or pretend that they have a feather) on the top of their hand. This will help with correct form.
- Practice conducting in both accented and legato styles. Ask the students to listen as you play the conducting section of the music. They are to be "music detectives," listening carefully and raising their hand or standing up to indicate when they hear the music change from the accented/sharp style to the legato style.
- **Bubble #4**: Does it sound like the music is growing louder? What do you call it when the music gets louder and louder? (Crescendo) How can you show what a crescendo is with your arms or your body? Does it look like an alligator's open

mouth when you see it on the music map? Can the students make that same shape using their arms? What happens after the crescendo? Can you follow the squiggles with your finger?

- **Bubble #5**: (The entire bubble repeats twice.) What do the students hear repeating at the beginning of this section? Which part sounds like the beginning of the song? (How are you, how are you.)
- Using the music map, show the students that two of Mozart's composer friends are asking each other: "How are you, how are you?" (four times) and then continuing on to sing "How are you, how are you, Mr. Mozart? Your music is the best!" What dynamic level did they use when they sang this part? (Forté)

I recommend stopping the CD after Bubble #5. Discuss Bubble #6 separately before playing the music for it.

- **Bubble #6**: Ask the students to listen, without looking at the music map, as you play Bubble #6 for them. Ask them to draw what they hear in the air. After this section is completed, stop the music and discuss why they felt the music should look like that.
- Look at Bubble #6 on the music map. Were their visual representations of the music accurate? Listen together, asking the students to follow the map in the air as you conduct through the map, using nonsense syllables.
- Work through Bubble #6 section by section. (Descending patterns interrupted by "How do you do?", followed by another descending pattern, two more "How do you do's" and then fast, swirling, music (You can say, "Circle, circle, circle," for this part) with two final-sounding chords at the end.

Introduce the music map

Using the music map, review from the beginning, stopping after Bubble #6. Ask the students to conduct in the air as you direct them through the map.

If time permits, have a few different students conduct (with your assistance).

Lesson Two

Objective
To add non-pitched percussion instruments to "Symphony no. 40." To secure the students' ability to follow the bubble chart of the symphony.

Previous Knowledge
Students should have reviewed through the first portion of the symphony, and should be able to follow the bubble map up to Bubble #6.

Materials required
CD, non-pitched percussion instruments, music map.

Suggested Teaching Process
- Review through the map together.
- Place the students into small groups: each group represents a specific bubble.

Sing, Act, Move and Play to the Bubbles!
(Please use this activity to your discretion, and adapt it to fit your classroom needs.)
- Divide the class into six equal groups, and ask each group to be in charge of representing a specific bubble. They will be presenting their bubble to the rest of the class after the designated practice time (usually ten minutes.)
- Make it clear to students that their job is to decide how they would like to represent their bubble. Remind students that they can sing, play, act, or dance out their bubble for the final presentation. You will be acting as a guide, walking from group to group, assisting groups with decision-making, teamwork, ideas, etc.

Perform the bubbles to the music. Ask each group to take a seat on the floor, and be prepared to rise and perform their bubble as it is played in the recording. First use the track with the lyrics and then just with the orchestral accompaniment.

Suggested Instrumentation

Depending on your class, you may choose to designate the groups' roles as indicated below:

Group 1: In charge of singing/acting out Bubble #1.

Group 2: Performs *accented conducting* pattern with *claves*. (Bubbles #2, #6)

Group 3: Performs *legato conducting pattern*, gliding fingernails in a two-beat conducting pattern on the hand drum, and using maracas for *creating crescendos*. (Bubbles #3, #4)

Group 4: Performs markings after crescendos, with cabasa(s) and rhythm sticks.

Group 5: Marks descending runs with jingle bells. (Bubbles #4, #6)

Group 6: Performs circle motion with fingernails on the drum. (Bubble #6)

You will need to try this at least a few times with the students, making sure to always have the chart in full view so they know where they are.

38

Persian March
(Sneaky Sam)
MUSIC: J. STRAUSS; MUSIC MAP: D. ZIOLKOSKI

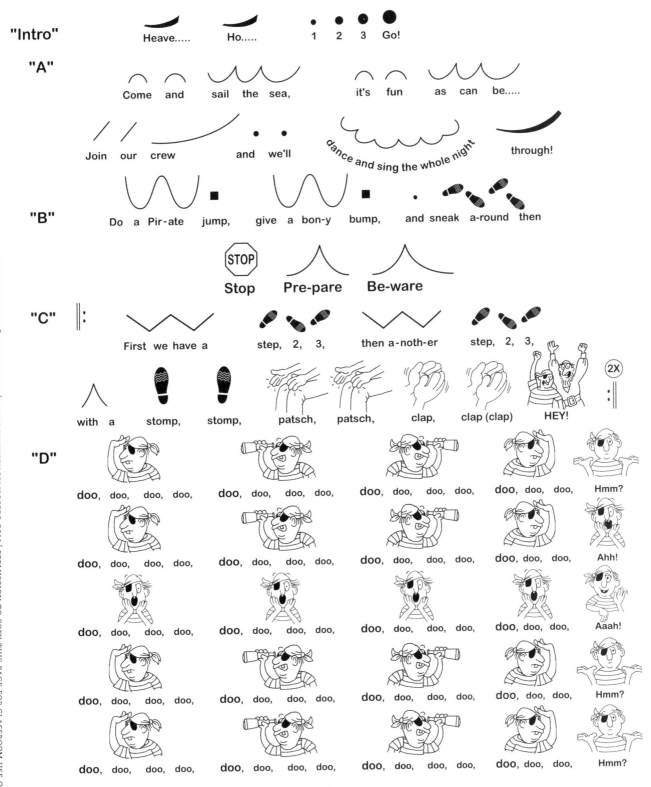

Final Form: intro A B C D intro A B C

Persian March

(Sneaky Sam)

MUSIC: J. STRAUSS; ARR./LYRICS: D. ZIOLKOSKI

TRIO D

Final form: Intro A B C D Intro A B C

Persian March

(Sneaky Sam)

MUSIC: J. STRAUSS

Goal

To familiarize children with the "Persian March" music by J. Strauss. Students will be able to sing and dance along to the music, conduct and recognize different sections on the music map.

Related Concepts

Phrasing, dynamics, forté and piano.

Recommended Grade: kindergarten–grade 6

Formation

Students are in a scattered formation for the entire song, with the exception of the first introduction (refer to end of Lesson One).

Materials required

Class-sized music map, CD, hand drum (if available).

The Sneaky Sam

A long time ago, there were many pirate ships that used to sail the seas searching for hidden treasures! One of the most famous ships of all was the Sneaky Sam.

Why was it called the Sneaky Sam? It was a very sneaky ship! None of the other pirate ships could figure out when or how the Sneaky Sam was able to sneak so many pirates aboard! Its crew seemed to grow and grow, almost like magic!

It wasn't really magic though, for late at night while the other crews were sleeping on their ships, the Sneaky Sam would pull up its anchor and sneak ashore to try and get new people to join their crew.

They would row very quietly so none of the other ships could hear. When they would get to shore they would start to sing and dance to their favourite pirate tune, the "Persian March."

People from the little towns close by would be woken from their sleeps by the sound of laughing, dancing pirates. They would light their candles, and walk down to the seashore in their pajamas.

This song was so much fun, that everyone would come. Big, grumpy men, old grandmothers, little girls and boys, and dainty little ladies would soon join the party. They would all sing and dance through the night, until the sun came up.

The Sneaky Sam didn't want the other pirate ships to know their secret to getting so many pirates. For this reason, they would invite all the people from the town who loved to sing and dance to row back to the middle of the sea before any of the other pirate ships woke from their long night's rest.

It was a wonderful crew! They worked together very well, almost like best friends do. They found more treasures than any other ship because they were such a hard working team.

The crew was so large that they were never really scared of anything while at sea, except of course for the Bad Bart. The Bad Bart was a pirate ship which had very mean, terrible pirates who *loved* to fight!

The pirates of the Sneaky Sam did not really know how to fight, and certainly did not want to learn. They were good, kind pirates. Meeting up with the Bad Bart pirates was a scary thought.

What would happen if they did meet up with them at sea? Nobody knows for sure, but I am sure you will find out if you join the crew of the Sneaky Sam.

If you are up late at night, and are listening closely, you might hear the pirates of the Sneaky Sam singing their favourite tune on the seashore. Make sure you wake up your mom and dad, and together you can go down to the seashore and join the pirates' party.

Would you like to learn the secret song of the Sneaky Sam? Maybe they will ask you to join their pirate crew!

Lesson One

Objective
Read the story and teach sections A, B, and C.

Suggested Teaching Process
For teachers who do not have instruments at their disposal, it is recommended that you teach this piece section by section. First introduce the story, and then teach the lyrics by rote. When the children are secure with this, add in suggested movements/actions. (Refer to the end of the lesson for an overview of recommended movements/ actions).

*Encourage students to improvise and add in their own movements when possible. When students are familiar with the song and movements, invite them to conduct along the music map with you as you demonstrate how the music follows the lines and squiggles shown on the map.

- Begin by telling students the story of the Sneaky Sam. Explain to students that it was because of the famous song and dance they did, that they were so successful in convincing so many people from the villages to join their crew.
- Invite students onto the floor. Warm up with some basic movement cues such as walking, hopping, jumping, skipping, etc. (Refer to the "Let's Warm Up" section found at the beginning of the book.)
- Once students are warmed up, play the marching stimulus on the hand drum, asking students to experiment walking in all different styles and directions.
- Play the marching signal for four beats, giving a quick tap before the fourth beat. Ask students to change directions every time they hear this quick tap. Try this a few times until the students feel secure.

- When they feel secure, ask the students if they can march to the right, and then turn/pivot and march to the left as you accompany them on the hand drum. When they are secure with this, ask them to place that section in their memory banks. (This movement will accompany the lyrics, "Come and sail the sea, it's fun as can be.")
- Introduce the skipping stimulus. If students are not familiar with this stimulus, use the discovery method to see if they can come up with the "skip" on their own as you play the stimulus on the hand drum. (Refer to "Let's Warm Up" at the beginning of the book.) *You may like to give them a hint by telling them that it is a step-hop combination.*
- When they discover the skip and are comfortable skipping around the room, ask them to listen as you play it six times, ending on an accented beat (the jumping stimulus) which serves as a half note.
- What could they do on that loud sound? Ask students to show you what they think it might be. (Children seem to naturally respond by jumping.) Can they jump like a pirate might? Play the skipping/jumping combination again, asking students to move as you play, remembering to land in a pirate jump!
- Combine the marching movement previously learned with the skipping/jump combination. Play it on the hand drum as children first listen, and then invite them to move as you play this Section A second time.
- Ask students to take a seat on the floor, inviting them to listen to your song. Sing the first section (up to the word "through") for the students. Teach this section of the melody by rote.
- Ask students to listen as you play the movement stimuli previously learned while you sing. (SEE FIGURE #1)

FIGURE #1

march right	Come	and	sail the	sea,	*march left*	It's	fun	as can	be
hand drum	S	S	S	S		S	S	S	S

- Demonstrate how to move hands for "Join our crew". Extend right hand outward with palm up, and then left hand. Tell students that you will represent this movement by two taps on the triangle. (Play on the words "join" and "crew".) Play the skipping stimuli, asking students to explore different movements if they are not certain of the stimulus.

  Guide students towards a skip by breaking the movement down to a step-hop. When students have discovered the skip, have them skip around the area they are in, landing with two feet on the word through. Try both parts together. (SEE FIGURE #2)

Section B

- Play the jumping stimuli again, asking students to show you their special pirate jump. Sing "Give a bon-y bump" while playing a tap on the cowbell on the word "bump". Demonstrate by moving your hip to the side on "bump". Demonstrate singing and dancing through the phrase. Ask students to join you the second time.*there is no movement on "do a pirate" or "give a bon-y" (SEE FIGURE #3)
- Tap lightly for five beats that accompany "And sneak around then Stop", beginning to tap on the word "Sneak" ("and" is an upbeat) and giving an accented tap on "Stop". What might a "sneaking pirate" look like? Ask students to show you as you sing this part for them. (SEE FIGURE #4)

- Ask students what types of voices they would like to use on words "Prepare" and "Beware"? Would they be soft and gentle voices, or loud and powerful? What could they do to make these words sound loud and powerful? (yell them out…perhaps by cupping hands around mouth!) This is a great time to reinforce the dynamic "forté".
- Try this section together. Play on drum while students move. (SEE FIGURE #5)
- Review from the beginning of the music while singing and dancing along with the students. (You might like to try up to this point with the CD)

Introduce Section C

Ask students to listen as you sing the words:
"First we have a step, 2, 3, then another step, 2, 3, with a stomp, stomp, patsch, patsch clap, clap "HEY"

- Ask students how they think they could move to words like these? Explore different possibilities. (I found that simply moving to the right eight steps worked best.) *There is no movement on words "First we have a"
- If they didn't figure out the stomp, stomp, patsch, patsch, clap, clap, Hey, part on their own, demonstrate on the spot by stomping right then left, patsching (slapping your thighs) for two beats, then clapping your own hands twice.
- Ask the students how they could make the word "Hey" sound super strong? (Yell hey, in a loud voice with arms extended upwards. I do this

FIGURE #2

	Join our r. hand	crew – l. hand	and we'll	dance skip	and skip	sing skip	the skip	whole skip	night skip	through jump

FIGURE #3

non-pitched percussion	Do	a	pi-rate	jump, X	give	a	bony	bump X

FIGURE #4

hand drum	And	sneak S	a- S	roound S	then S	stop S

FIGURE #5

hand drum	And	sneak S	a- S	roound S	then S	stop, S	Pre-pare – Be-ware – (call out)

facing forward.) Let children imagine that they are loud and boisterous pirates here, shouting "HEY" at a fortissimo dynamic. (ff)

• The second time they sing/move through that part, they are to *move to the left and add in one extra clap.*

• If time permits, add in the instrumental accompaniment for sections A, B, and C. Review from the beginning, sing, dancing and playing through up to section C, first on your own and then with the CD.

Suggested instrumentation
(Refer to Suggested Movement/Actions or the music for rhythmic notation of the phrases below)

Section A
1. Claves/rhythm sticks: "Come and sail the seas, its fun as can be"
2. Triangle: "Join our Crew"
3. Temple Blocks: "Dance and sing the whole night through" (skipping stimulus played on the beat)

Section B
4. Bass drum: "jump"
5. Cow bell/agogo bells: "bump"
6. Sand blocks: (and) "sneak a-round then stop"

Section C
7. Claves/rhythm sticks: "Step, 2, 3, then another, step 2, 3,"
8. Hand drum: "stomp, stomp"
9. Guiro: "patsch patsch"
10. Finger Cymbals: "clap clap"
11. Tambourine: "Hey" (tambourine)

Section D
12. Cabassa: "doo,doo,doos"

Special Introduction: "Tug of War"
• Invite students to find a spot on the floor. Tell them that you are going to make the introduction special, by pretending that they are playing a game of tug-of-war with one of the large ropes from the sails.

• Ask students to make a line, with half the team pretending to pull the rope one way on the word "heave", the others the other way on "Ho" and then running about in a scattered position on "1, 2, 3, Go". On the second introduction, students can just pretend to play tug-of-war from the spot they are at.

Introduce the Music Map
• Have students join you in front of the large music map. While listening to the CD, review sections A, B, and C from the beginning. Conduct the music map as students conduct in the air using their conducting finger.

• Ask one volunteer who was accurately following the music map to guest conduct (remember the top-hat and special conducting baton).

Lesson Two

Objectives
Introduce section D. Sing, dance and play through entire selection.

Suggested Teaching Process
Review through sections A, B, and C by singing and dancing through the parts to the CD accompaniment. Continue on with section "D".

Section D: Let's Improvise!
(Refer to music for rhythmic notation)
• Explain to students that in this next section, the pirates were all keeping watch on deck, looking for any pirate ships, treasures or islands that might be nearby. While looking, they sang.

• Demonstrate for students, being extra dramatic for effect. {refer to music for melody line, or sing along with the CD} (SEE FIGURE #6)

FIGURE #6

Doo,	doo,	doo,	doo,	**doo,**	doo,	doo,	doo,
(look)				*(look)*			
Doo,	doo,	doo,	doo,	**doo,**	doo,	doo,	**Hmm?**
(look)				*(look)*			*(shrug)*

45

- Tell students that the pirates shrugged their shoulders because they were not able to find anything or anyone…They were puzzled, but they kept on looking.
- Ask students to watch as you demonstrate phrase one through the first time. Tell them that they will join you and the other crew members the second time through. Invite students to help you search the seas, by looking through their telescopes for other pirate ships, treasures etc.
- Encourage students to use different levels when doing this. Look high, then, low, in every direction, this will encourage students to make use of their space and to be very dramatic.

While students are singing along on doo, doo doo,…I often make up little things to say in a pirate type of voice. (Ahoy mates! Shiver me timbers. You can ask different students to try this every time you sing through the piece. This is a great opportunity for solo improvisation)

- Demonstrate the second phrase. Pretend you have spotted a very scary pirate ship called the "Bad Bart" gasping "Ahhh" and then pretending to shake in fear on the "doos" that follow. (strike a scared pose on each of the accented/bold "doos") (SEE FIGURES #7 AND #8)
- Continue on pretending to search for other ships or treasures. (SEE FIGURES #9 AND #10)
- Practice singing and dancing through Section D with the CD accompaniment. When secure, invite students to join you in front of the class sized music map.

Conduct through entire selection on the music map
- Ask the students to listen to the "Persian March" on the CD, while singing quietly, and conducting in the air, as you guide them along by following along on the music map.
- Ask if there are any volunteers who would like to conduct through the class music map (with your guidance.)
- Review from the beginning.
*On the *second introduction* have students maneuver the rope on "Heave Ho" from their present location. On "1, 2, 3, Go", they can just indicate the counts by looking sharply around the room on the counts.

FIGURE #7

Doo,	doo,	doo,	doo,	**doo,**	doo,	doo,	doo,
(look)				(look)			
Doo,	doo,	doo,	doo,	**doo,**	doo,	doo,	**Aaah!**
(look)				(look)			(scared gasp)

FIGURE #8

| **Doo,** | doo, | doo, | doo, | **doo,** | doo, | doo, | doo, |
| (make a frightened pose on the strong beats, the bold "doos," |
| **Doo,** | doo, | doo, | doo, | **doo,** | doo, | doo, | **Aaah!** |
| and then say "ahhh" as if you don't care about spotting Bad Bart) |

FIGURE #9

Doo,	doo,	doo,	doo,	**doo,**	doo,	doo,	doo,
(look)				(look)			
Doo,	doo,	doo,	doo,	**doo,**	doo,	doo,	**Hmm?**
(look)				(look)			(shrug)

FIGURE #10

Doo,	doo,	doo,	doo,	**doo,**	doo,	doo,	doo,
(look)				(look)			
Doo,	doo,	doo,	doo,	**doo,**	doo,	doo,	**Hmm?**
(look)				(look)			(shrug)

46

Summary of Suggested Movements/Actions

Introduction: "Tug of War" positioning

Section A

march right

s   s   s   s

Come   and   sail the   sea,

march left

s   s   s   s

it's   fun   as can   be.

Join   our   crew   and we'll

*(right hand out on "join,"   (no movement)
left hand out on "crew")*

s   r   s   r   s   r   s   r

Dance   and   sing   the

s   r   s   r   S

whole   night   through!

Skip around room starting on word "dance" and freezing in a pirate position on the word "through". Tell students to put the story in their eyes, and pretend to search around the room during this longer note.)

Section B

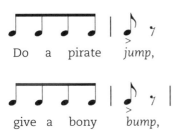

Do   a   pirate   jump,

give   a   bony   bump,

(Students give their best version of a pirate jump on the word "jump", and then thrust their hip out to the side, or to another partner, on the word "bump." No movement on "do a pirate" or "give a bony.")

s   s   s   s   s

And sneak a-   round   then   STOP

(call out in a pirate voice)
PRE-PARE, BE-WARE...

(Tiptoe around in a sneaking manner, then on words "Prepare", "Beware" shout out with hands cupped around mouth in shouting manner.)

Section C

march right

s   s   s   s

First we have a step,   2,   3,   then another

s   s   s   s

step,   2,   3,   with a

s   s   s   s

step,   2,   3,   with a

face front

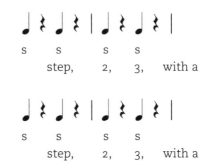

Stomp, stomp,   patsch, patsch

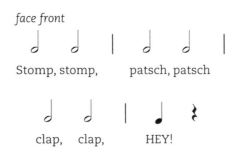

clap,   clap,   HEY!

(Repeat "First we have a..." section, but moving left the second time. There is also an extra clap at the end: "clap, clap, clap, HEY!")

Section D Improvise
Act like pirates searching for ships or treasures.
(Every 4 beats look in a new direction.)

1.

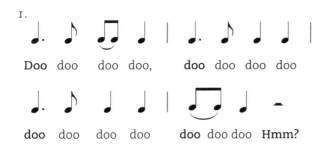

Doo doo   doo doo,   **doo** doo doo doo

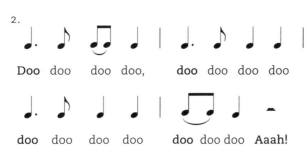

doo doo   doo doo   **doo** doo doo **Hmm?**

2.

doo doo   doo doo   **doo** doo doo **Aaah!**

3.

Doo doo   doo doo,   **doo** doo doo doo

doo   doo   doo doo   **doo** doo doo **Ahhh!**

4.

Doo doo   doo doo,   **doo** doo doo doo

doo   doo   doo doo   **doo** doo doo **Hmm?**

5.

Doo doo   doo doo,   **doo** doo doo doo

doo   doo   doo doo   **doo** doo doo **Hmm?**

Final Form: Intro A B C D intro A B C

48

Fossils

MUSIC: C. SAINT-SAËNS; MUSIC MAP: D. ZIOLKOSKI

Tapping Sheet

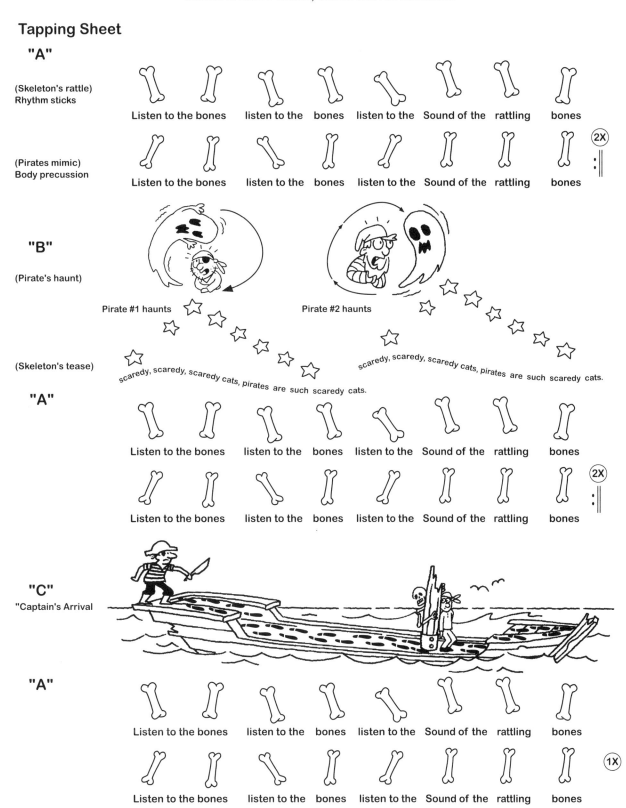

"A"

(Skeleton's rattle)
Rhythm sticks

Listen to the bones   listen to the   bones   listen to the   Sound of the   rattling   bones

(Pirates mimic)
Body precussion

Listen to the bones   listen to the   bones   listen to the   Sound of the   rattling   bones   2X

"B"

(Pirate's haunt)

Pirate #1 haunts   Pirate #2 haunts

(Skeleton's tease)

scaredy, scaredy, scaredy cats, pirates are such scaredy cats.

scaredy, scaredy, scaredy cats, pirates are such scaredy cats.

"A"

Listen to the bones   listen to the   bones   listen to the   Sound of the   rattling   bones

Listen to the bones   listen to the   bones   listen to the   Sound of the   rattling   bones   2X

"C"
"Captain's Arrival"

"A"

Listen to the bones   listen to the   bones   listen to the   Sound of the   rattling   bones

Listen to the bones   listen to the   bones   listen to the   Sound of the   rattling   bones   1X

Final Form: Rondo A B A C A

Fossils

MUSIC: C. SAINT-SAËNS; ARR./LYRICS: D. ZIOLKOSKI

* Sections in brackets are spoken

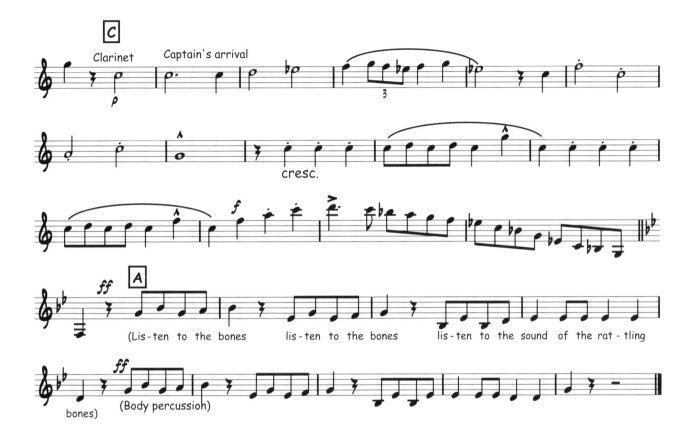

Fossils

MUSIC: C. SAINT-SAËNS

Goal
To familiarize students with the music "Fossils" by Camille Saint-Saëns. Students will sing, dance, and play to the music. Students will identify different sections of this rondo, and be able to follow along on the music map.

Related Concepts
Rondo form, phrasing.

Recommended Grade: grade 4+

Suggested themes
Halloween/pirates/skeletons

Formation
Scattered, and then in a circle.

Materials required
Rhythm sticks (if available), music map.

Lesson One

Objective
To read the story aloud, and sing, dance, and play through Section A.

Suggested Teaching Process
Begin by discussing the significance of a fossil. What exactly is a fossil? Explain that a fossil is a bone or skeletal part that has turned to stone over many years. Ask students where they might see fossils.

Story-time
Read the story to the students after reviewing the plans that follow. Note: The words in parenthesis are meant to facilitate the teacher for future reference.

Voyage on the High "C's"

Many years ago, there was a pirate ship that sailed the seas in search of the missing music of a very famous composer, Camille Saint-Saëns.

Captain James manned the helm as his crew of burly pirates worked on deck. Night after night they searched the seas for the infamous ship that was said to have stolen the music and then crashed into a rocky cliff long ago.

Rumour was that it was now a ghost ship haunted by the phantoms of its pirate crew. On dark nights you could hear their skeletons dancing on deck, and the hollow laughter that could make the hairs on your arm stand on end.

Nonetheless, this did not deter the brave crew of Captain James. They were very determined to recover the music, and promised they'd never quit their search!

One night during a fierce storm, Captain James's ship crashed right into the jagged remains of the old pirate ship. Too nervous to explore the ship at that late midnight hour, Captain James decided that they would have to wait until morning.

His crew, however, was too curious and intrigued by rumours of the dancing skeletons and haunted ship. Daring and taunting each other, Captain James's crew stepped aboard to investigate, unbeknownst to their beloved captain.

To their disbelief, the first sounds they heard were the rattling of skeleton's bones.

(Demonstrate section A's pattern on rhythm sticks.)
Skeleton's Rattle: (SEE FIGURE #1)

FIGURE #1

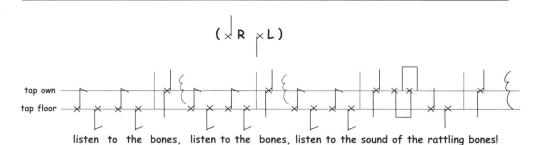

listen to the bones, listen to the bones, listen to the sound of the rattling bones!

Thinking someone was just tricking them, the pirates mimicked the same rhythmic pattern back, almost daring the skeletons to rattle their bones again!

(Demonstrate pattern using body percussion.)
Pirates' Mimic: (SEE FIGURE #2)

The pirates quickly realized that there were a few of them who were truly scared, so they began to taunt and tease each other.

(Section B, pirates haunting: First eight beats, Pirate 1 pretends to be a ghost and scare Pirate 2; the second eight beats, Pirate 2 makes fun of Pirate 1.)

The skeletons decided to tease the pathetically frightened "brave" pirates by boldly skipping forward out and around the pirates. The pirates were too shocked to move!

(Skeletons' Tease: Skeletons skip around the pirates singing: "Scaredy, scaredy, scardey cats! Pirates are such scaredy cats!" (2x))

The skeletons were having so much fun, that they decided to rattle their bones once again. The pirates were determined not to show their fear, and echoed back relentlessly. What a racket they created!
Hearing all the commotion, Captain James decides to investigate. Hearing the captain's footsteps approaching, the pirates and skeletons both freeze in hopes of not being caught!

Section C: Captain's Arrival

(Designated student struts around the ship acting like the "captain," looking to see what all the noise is about. Unable to see anything, he retires back to his own ship so he can sleep.)

Not wanting the fun to end, the skeletons and pirates played their little game for a final time, rattling and mimicking the sounds of rattling bones!

As for the pirates, they ended up fleeing the wreckage, as the skeletons were victorious in scaring them away. To this day, if you listen closely you can hear the skeletons singing and dancing to "Fossils," their all-time favourite music!

Section A: Skeleton's Rattle

(First phrase, Section A performed on rhythm sticks.)

- Teach Section A.
- Have students sit cross-legged facing you, each with a pair of rhythm sticks.
- Demonstrate. (SEE FIGURE #3)
- Have the students echo you, playing back the phrase first in small segments, and then in its entirety.
- When they are secure, have the students sit in a few small circles and play the entire phrase.

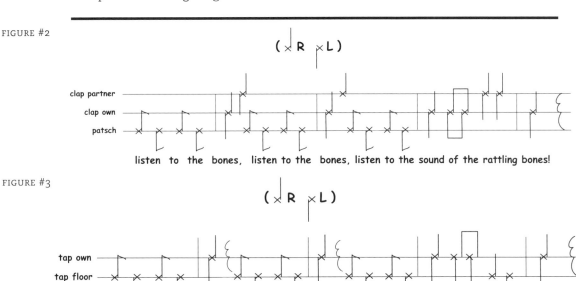

FIGURE #2

(R L)

clap partner
clap own
patsch

listen to the bones, listen to the bones, listen to the sound of the rattling bones!

FIGURE #3

(R L)

tap own
tap floor

listen to the bones, listen to the bones, listen to the sound of the rattling bones!

53

Section A: Pirates' Mimic
(Second phrase of Section A)

- Discuss how the pirates must have felt after hearing the rattling bones. (Scared.) How did they react? (They pretended they weren't scared, and made fun of the sounds by mimicking them back on their bodies).
- Demonstrate and have students echo back the body percussion version. (SEE FIGURE #4)
- For a challenge, after the word "bones," see if the students can clap their partner's hands. It must be a really quick clap. This works best with older students.
- Practice the entire phrase a few times saying the speech pattern while performing body percussion. Practice asking all students to face you, pretending that you are their partner. When they are secure with this, ask them to turn to the person next to them. Remember to say the phrase as you play it on your bodies.

To insure all students are secure, and to make it fun, after the students perform the body percussion 2x with a partner, say, "Switch." Tell them that you (or a designated student) will then play the entire rhythm 2x on the temple blocks. They have this amount of time to find a new partner.

- Using the formation suggested below, divide students into two groups, skeletons and pirates (pirates being in partners), and try the entire Section A. Switch sections if time permits.

Formation

- **Skeleton Group** sits in a small circle (in the middle of the floor) with rhythm sticks.
- **Pirate Group** pirates are paired off in partners and make a larger circle around the skeleton group. Partners are facing each other for the body percussion.

Lesson Two

Objective
Teach sections B and C, and review through in their entirety.

Section B: "Pirates' Scare and Skeletons' Tease" Let's Improvise!

- Have students listen to Section B in the music. Ask if they can hear where the pirates are moving around each other acting like ghosts trying to scare each other?
- What could possibly be happening when the "Twinkle Twinkle Little Star" theme starts? *(Skeletons are mocking the scared pirates, who are acting like scared children. They skip around the pirates in a child like way, and return to their spot at the end of the phrase).*
- Keeping the same two groups and formation that you had with Section A, have pirates improvise ghostlike movements, teasing each other. (Creatively move around each other for eight beats each for a total of sixteen beats.) Try with the music.
- Keeping sticks discreetly in hands, skeletons then boldly skip around the pirates, looking at them as if they were young children. Demonstrate, singing aloud, "Scaredy, scaredy, scaredy cats! Pirates are such scaredy cats!" (2x)
- Tell the students that the skeletons must return back to their inner circle by the end of the theme. Teach students this small melody by rote, and then ask them to try skipping around the pirates as you help them sing.
- Try it from the very beginning using the first track of "Fossils" (with lyrics to help guide students).

FIGURE #4

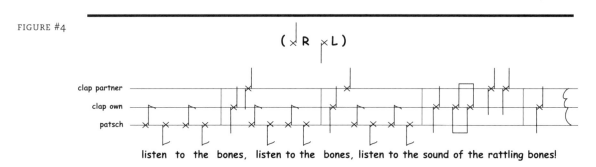

listen to the bones, listen to the bones, listen to the sound of the rattling bones!

Section C: Captain's Arrival

- Ask students if they recall what happened in Section C. (Captain James came aboard the Ghost Ship to investigate what all the commotion was about. Since it was dark, he strolled across the deck unable to detect the pirates and skeletons that stood frozen in their places. The captain then returned back to his ship where he went back to sleep.)
- First, listen to the music for Section C, and ask students what type of mood they feel it sets. (Happy, proud, curious…) Ask students if they could act out how the captain might be strutting about the ship to this music. Ask students for a volunteer to play the role of the captain for Section C.
- Review with the students what the pirates and skeletons are doing at this time. (Frozen in their places.) Keep the same groups as were determined in Section A.
- Ask students to get into their positions (skeletons in the inner circle, pirates in partners surrounding them, and the selected captain ready to stroll about). Play the music having students act out their parts.
- Review the form with the students, talking through how they would need to move through each section. Ask students to get into their positions, and take it from the beginning. Switch parts allowing students to experience being both the pirates and the skeletons. Have fun!

What is a Rondo?

- Discuss what a rondo is. Explain to students that it is like a musical club sandwich. The piece of bread is represented by Section A, and then some meat might be placed on it (Section B), followed by another piece of bread (Section A), and then perhaps some cheese (Section C), and then topped with a last piece of bread (Section A).
- Write out the form on the board: A B A C A. Is this a rondo? (Yes.) Discuss what's happening in the story with each of the sections. You may like to refer back to the story and have students come up with the events of each section.
- A: Skeletons' dance, then pirates' mimic.
- B: Pirates tease each other pretending to be ghosts, and then on "Twinkle Twinkle Little Star" theme, the skeletons make fun of them and boldly skip around the pirates.
- C: The captain awakens from his sleep, and investigates the noise aboard the wreckage (pirates and skeletons freeze, not wanting to get caught).
- Listen to track #9 of "Fossils." This will reinforce the sequence of events.

55

Aquarium
(The Giant Octopus)
MUSIC: C. SAINT-SAËNS; MUSIC MAP: D. ZIOLKOSKI

"A" Sea creatures swim around Octopus.

"B" Giant octopus is scared and moves down to the ocean floor

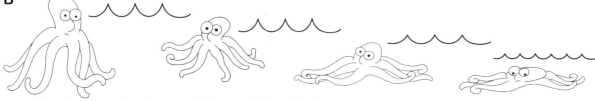

"C" Creatures swim closer and closer to the Giant

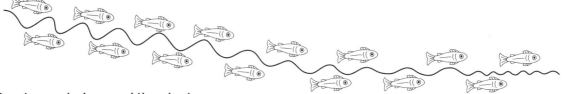

"D" Creatures circle round the giant

Repeat A B C

"E" Giant octopus lashes out   sea creatures swim back slowly.

"F" Sea creatures swim away leaving the Giant alone.

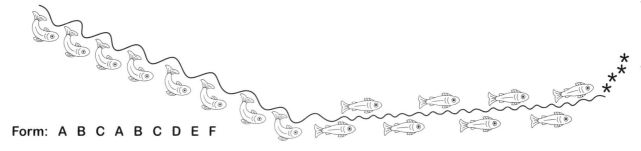

Form: A B C A B C D E F

Aquarium
(The Giant Octopus)

MUSIC: C. SAINT-SAËNS; MUSIC MAP: D. ZIOLKOSKI

Form: A B C A B C D E F

Aquarium
(The Giant Octopus)
MUSIC: CAMILLE SAINT-SAËNS

Goal
To familiarize children with "Aquarium" by Saint-Saëns. Through the aid of a story, children will move creatively to the music. Students will be able to distinguish between various sections of the music and follow the music map successfully.

Related Concepts
Identify high to low through movement and music. Smooth "legato" vs. short and choppy (staccato) sound qualities, descending music patterns.

Recommended Grade: grades 2+

Suggested Themes
Fish/Ocean

Formation
Scattered

Materials required
Scarves or long, light strips of material, music map, picture books of the ocean and/or sea creatures. (Non-pitched percussion instruments are required for movement warm-up activity.)

Lesson One

Objective
To discuss sea creatures and how they move in the water. Read or look at a few picture books with sea creatures from the ocean to help stimulate the children's imagination. Students will move creatively as sea creatures to the music "Aquarium."

Suggested Teaching Process
- Discuss what types of creatures are found in the sea. Which of these creatures may be kept in an aquarium? How big can aquariums be?
- Stimulate their imaginations by looking through some of the illustrations in books. "Fishes" by Brian Wildsmith is a great book to start with.

- Discuss the way fish move in the water. Some questions you may like to ask are: Do fish move in a choppy manner or do they swim quite smoothly? How does it feel when you move through the water?

Movement Warm-Up
- Play a cymbal with a mallet. What type of sound is this? Smooth or choppy? Does it last for a long time or short? (Ask students to move about the room as they listen to the smooth, sustained tone of the cymbal. Have students freeze when the sound dies off.)
- Remind students to think about using their high, medium, and low levels with their bodies.
- Add in scarves and/or ribbon sticks
- Dim or shut off your lights, leaving just enough natural light to set the mood for a deep-water scene. Have students listen to the instrumental version of "Aquarium" on the CD. Ask students to move creatively in the water as discussed above. What types of creatures are they? (Have fun guessing as students pretend to be creatures in the sea.)
- If available, add in ribbon sticks and/or scarves to imitate the beautiful, colourful fins, tails, and other fish parts moving through the water.

Lesson Two

Objective
Read the story "The Giant Octopus" to the children. Creatively move through the music as octopus or sea creatures. Conduct through the music map, and distinguish the difference between sections.

Story-time
Engage your students in an intriguing story that they can creatively move to!

The Giant Octopus

In the dark depths of the sea lived a very large, oversized octopus. Every creature feared him, including the many scuba divers who managed to swim down far enough to catch a glimpse of him. To mankind, he was considered to be a mystical legend as very few people really believed a creature so great in size could really exist.

Due to his size, he was often alone. Most sea creatures feared him and would usually swim away if the octopus tried to approach them. They judged him on size alone, and never once gave the octopus a chance to be a part of their underwater world.

They would often gather in large schools to try to scare the giant octopus, wishing that it would leave their little area. They felt that the giant octopus was getting too much attention from the world above, which worried and scared all the other fish. This made them feel like they were in danger as well.

One night, all the creatures from the sea that lived near the giant octopus met to develop a plan. They wanted to figure out a way to scare away the giant octopus so that he would never return.

After some time, the sea creatures felt certain that they could convince the "giant" to leave with their creative plan. Would you like to dive down into the deep ocean water to visit the giant octopus? Put your scuba gear on, and let's dive in!

Suggested Teaching Process: Creative Movement
- Invite students onto the floor (ocean floor) in a scattered form:
- Brainstorm with students how a giant octopus could be formed using a small group of students. After discussing different possibilities, divide students into small groups (each group having at least one or two strong leaders) and ask them to create their own special giant octopus. Walk around from group to group assisting students when necessary.
- After students have established how they are going to create their octopus, ask them to listen as you sing the words, "See the giant, moving slowly, down towards the ground." (Refer to music or CD for assistance.)
- How can they make their octopus move from a high, to medium, to low, to ocean-floor position?

Ask various groups to demonstrate as you sing the melody (or play that specific section on the CD).
- Ask all the groups to demonstrate how their octopus moves as you sing the melody. This is like a "show and tell." Give students an opportunity to answer any questions from other students, and to talk about the composition of their giant octopus.
- Ask students if there is a group that would volunteer to be the giant octopus. Place this group in the center of the room.
- Divide other students into two equal groups, designating them as sea creature group 1 and sea creature group 2.
- While students are seated on the floor (either in the center as an octopus, or scattered randomly as a sea creature), ask them to listen as you play the first track of "Aquarium." Demonstrate Section A by moving around creatively as a sea creature. Explain to students that it is the sea creatures group 1 that moves first, and then they freeze as sea creatures group 2 moves to the second phrase.
- After you demonstrate Section A, ask the students to try moving around the room *with you*, while listening to that section of music. Stimulate the children's imagination by pretending to see all sorts of interesting creatures as you swim through the sea.
  This is a great time to positively reinforce children's creative movement abilities and improvisational skills.
- Repeat this same process with each of the sections below.
  As a teacher, you are always guiding and/or moving with whichever group is supposed to be moving.
- Tell students that when it is not their turn to move, they are to be in a frozen position.
- When you have moved through all the separate sections with the students, review from the beginning. If time permits, have students switch parts, sea creatures becoming the giant octopus and vice versa.

Use the music map to reinforce story and movements

- After students have moved through the entire selection, ask students to conduct along in the air as you conduct through the large music map. The first time through, use the recording with the lyrics (track 13). (Take time to discuss the significance of each section below before playing/conducting through the music. This will reinforce the sequence of events for the students).

Section A

Sea creatures are swimming around the giant octopus, checking him out. They are trying to warn the "giant," giving him the message that they want him to leave. (Remind students that sea creatures group 1 moves to the first phrase and then freezes, as sea creatures group 2 moves to the second phrase.)

Section B

The giant octopus then starts to descend, to move away from the sea creatures that are disturbing him. He moves from a high position, to a medium position, to a low position and then tries to hide on the ocean floor.

Section C

The sea creatures do not let him escape, and move closer to the giant continuing to keep a close watch on him.

Repeat sections A, B, and C again, then continue on with sections D, E, and F.

Section D

The sea creatures continue to swim around the giant octopus.

Section E

The giant octopus was feeling sad and scared, but he knew that he didn't do anything wrong. Acting very bravely, he refuses to let the sea creatures bother him, but he warns them with great whip like motions of his long yet powerful arms.

Not once or twice, but four great lashes. Every time he lashes out, the other creatures move back, amazed at how strong and brave the giant octopus is.

Section F

Finally, realizing that this great creature could have easily attacked them yet chose only to protect himself, the sea creatures had a new respect for this mysterious giant octopus, and left it alone in the very deep ocean water where they knew he would be happy.

As they swam away, they waved good-bye with their fins, which let the octopus know they were sorry bothering him.

After the students have experienced moving through both parts using the recording with the lyrics (track 13), ask students to internalize the lyrics and move through the piece using the instrumental recording (track 14).

Anitra's Dance

(Spy dance)

MUSIC E. GRIEG; MUSIC MAP: D. ZIOLKOSKI

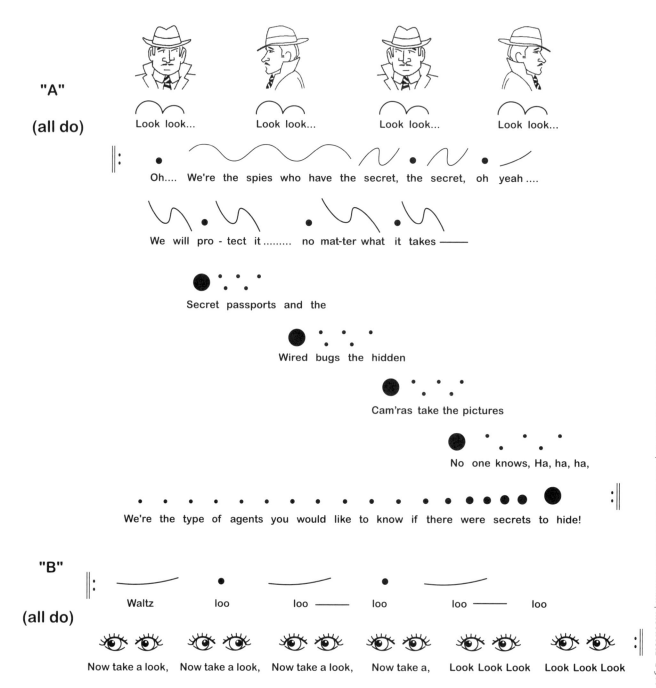

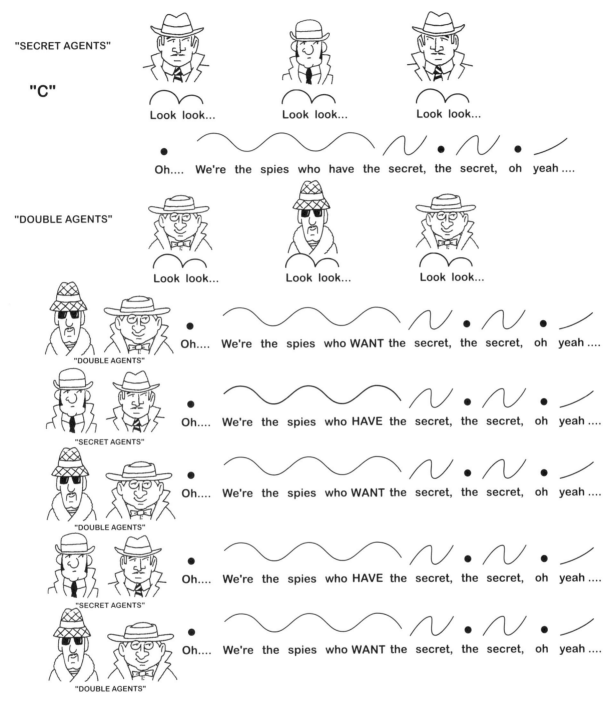

"SECRET AGENTS"

"C"

Look look... Look look... Look look...

Oh.... We're the spies who have the secret, the secret, oh yeah ....

"DOUBLE AGENTS"

Look look... Look look... Look look...

"DOUBLE AGENTS"

Oh.... We're the spies who WANT the secret, the secret, oh yeah ....

"SECRET AGENTS"

Oh.... We're the spies who HAVE the secret, the secret, oh yeah ....

"DOUBLE AGENTS"

Oh.... We're the spies who WANT the secret, the secret, oh yeah ....

"SECRET AGENTS"

Oh.... We're the spies who HAVE the secret, the secret, oh yeah ....

"DOUBLE AGENTS"

Oh.... We're the spies who WANT the secret, the secret, oh yeah ....

** Return to section "A" (all performing) with the small addition of
"We want to steal it, no matter what it takes"

Section "B" - remains as is.

Section "C" - remains as is.

Section "A*" - and spies flee the scene to hide.... on the last sounding note!

Final Form: A B C A* B C A*

Anitra's Dance
(Spy dance)
MUSIC E. GRIEG; ARR./LYRICS: D. ZIOLKOSKI

Final form: ABC A'BC A'

Anitra's Dance
(Spy dance)
MUSIC E. GRIEG

Goal
To familiarize students with "Anitra's Dance" by Edvard Grieg. Students will sing, dance, and move through the music. They will identify sections of the music, and conduct through the music map.

Related Concepts
Crescendo, decrescendo, contrasting dynamic levels throughout the piece (*ff* to *pp*).

Recommended Grade: grade 4+

Materials required
CD, music map.

The Quest for the Secret Formula

Many years ago, a secret agent team was sent on a secret mission to seek out a very important secret formula. This formula was said to make you disappear on command. The perfect formula for secret agents to own!

Little did they know that every secret agent team in the world was after the same secret formula. Even the infamous Double Agent team (who, as you know, have some of the best spies in the world) was searching for this formula.

The Secret Agent team knew that the sneaky Double Agent team was their greatest competition. They were determined to get their hands on that formula before they did!

Together they came up with a brilliant plan, a strategy that was certain to outsmart all the other agents and double agents around.

With a bit of luck, amazing skill and strategy, the Secret Agent team managed to find the formula. Placing it in a very sneaky place, they dressed up like tourists and caught a ride on the first cruise ship headed for their homeland. They were hoping to look like your typical tourist, on vacation and having fun. To celebrate their victory, they decided to dance up a storm!

While on the dance floor dancing the tango, they spotted other tourists who seemed a bit peculiar looking. Secret agents are trained to always be on the lookout, for they never knew who is watching or following them.

Could it be? Indeed it was! The dreaded Double Agent team! Feeling quite confident about their amazing hiding place for the secret formula, the secret agent team began to brag about their victory. They sang, "Oh we're the spies who *have* the secret, the secret, oh yeah!" The Double Agent team glared at them and sang back, "Oh we're the spies who *want* the secret, the secret, oh yeah!" The battle began!

Would you like to learn the "Spy Dance?" Maybe you too can become a secret agent, or perhaps a double agent!

66

Lesson One

Objective
To teach the movement and lyrics to Section A.

Suggested Teaching Process
Demonstrate Section A of the music, singing and dancing in front of students, acting like a secret agent.

Suggested Movement: Section A
All spies begin as secret agent members.
- *Introduction: students are in tango position, look sharply in different directions*
  Look, look,   Look, look,   Look, look,   Look, look
- *Tango right*
  Oh we're the spies who have the secret, the secret, oh yeah!
- *Tango Left*
  We will protect it, no matter what it takes.
- *Cross chest, right hand then left*
  Secret passports and the wired bugs.
- *Point to corner, shake finger right/left*
  The hidden cameras take pictures no one knows.
- *Throw head back in laughing manner*
  Ha, ha, ha!
- *Hands behind back and circle round*
  We're the type of agents you would like to know if there were secrets to hide!
On the word "hide" strike a secret spy pose.

- Teach the lyrics to Section A by rote, first just through speech. When the students are secure, add in the melody line. Ask the students to echo back to you, phrase by phrase. These words are difficult to sing at a quick tempo, so take your time reinforcing them by repetition.
- When the lyrics are fairly secure, invite the students onto the floor. Have them sing and dance along with you, first individually, and then in partners.
- Try Section A with the recording (track 13). Have students internalize the lyrics as they move to the instrumental version (track 14).

Lesson Two

Objective
To teach the song and movement for "Anitra's Dance" in its entirety. Students will be able to conduct through the music and identify specific sections of the music.

Suggested Teaching Process
- Review Section A of the music, first by singing through the music to review the lyrics. The second time, sing and dance through with a partner.
- Demonstrate Section B to students. Exaggerate movement, to add to the drama of the piece.

Suggested Movement for Section B
Waltz, loo, loo----, loo, loo----, loo,
(act very sophisticated)
Now take a look. Now take a look. Now take a look. Now take a look. Look, look, look, look, look, look, look.
(Look sharply, searching the room.)

Waltz, loo, loo----, loo, loo----, loo,
(act very sophisticated.)
Now take a look. Now take a look. Now take a look. Now take a look. Look, look, look, look, look, look, look.
(Look sharply, searching the room.)

- Ask students to try this with you. First individually, and then with partners. When they are comfortable with these movements, introduce Section C.

Section C

Divide the students into two teams: secret agents and double agents. Secret agent members begin while others are frozen:

"**Look** look,   **Look**, look,   **Look**, look."

- Tango one direction: "Oh we're the spies who **HAVE** the secret, the secret, oh yeah!" *Secret Agent members freeze.
- Double Agent members: "**Look**, look, **Look**, look, **Look**, look."
- Tango opposite direction: "Oh we're the spies who **WANT** the secret, the secret, oh yeah!" *Double Agent members freeze.
- Secret agents: Oh we're the spies who **HAVE** the secret (freeze).
- Double Agents: Oh we're the spies who **WANT** the secret (freeze).
- Secret agents: Oh we're the spies who **HAVE** the secret (freeze).
- Double Agents: Oh we're the spies who **WANT** the secret (freeze).

Repeat Section A, B, and a slightly shorter version of C. Return to Section A* for the final ending. When students hear the high-pitched note, have them scatter in different directions, as if running to hide from something, or someone. Watch out!

Helpful hints with movement:

Begin movement with a basic movement warm-up, as found in the "Let's Warm Up" section of the book. Students can discover the waltz step through the presentation of your hand drum stimuli. Indicate to students that when you tap the skin of the drum you would like them to take a step, and when you tap the rim, you would like them to go high up on their toes.

Remind students that usually the rim is used for the "hop" stimulus, but in this case it will be used to indicate high stepping on their toes. Step (tap drum), toe (tap rim), toe (tap rim). Ask students to practice their waltz by first trying it on their own, in all sorts of directions, and then, when they are secure, with a partner.

Section B

Waltz around freely, just making certain that by the end of Section B partners are back to their original starting positions.

Section C

Designate one half of the room as the Secret agent members, and the other half as the Double Agents. The Secret agent begin tangoing towards the Double Agents as they remain staying frozen, and then vice versa. The groups end up crossing through each other to get to the opposite side.

Repeat Sections A, B, and slightly shorter version of C from opposite sides of the room, as ended off with in Section C the first time through. Return to Section A* (modified version of "A," with the addition of "we're going to steal it, no matter what it takes). At the end of this section students will run off to hide in all different directions at the sound of the high pitched note.

Sing, dance and act through "Anitra's Dance" with the assistance of the CD. Try using first the track with the lyrics and then the instrumental version. When the students are secure with this, introduce the music map to them.

Introduce the music map

- Invite the students join you in front of the large music map. While listening to the CD, review through the entire selection.
- Conduct the class music map as students conduct in the air using their conducting finger.
- Ask one volunteer who was accurately following the music map to guest conduct (remember the top-hat and special conducting baton).

Hungarian Dance no. 5

MUSIC: J. BRAHMS; MUSIC MAP: D. ZIOLKOSKI

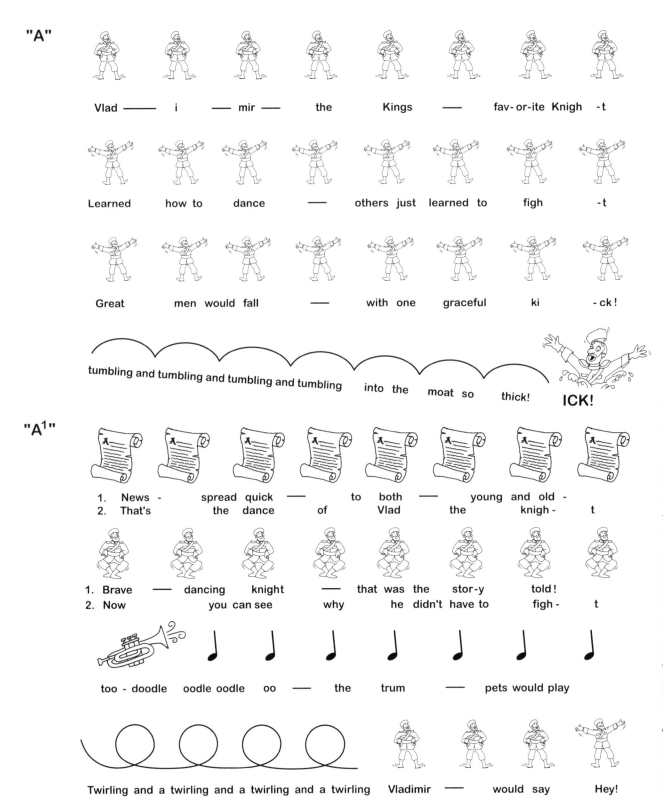

"A"

Vlad —— i — mir — the   Kings —— fav-or-ite Knigh -t

Learned   how to   dance —— others just learned to   figh   -t

Great   men would fall —— with one   graceful   ki   - ck !

tumbling and tumbling and tumbling and tumbling   into the   moat so   thick!   ICK!

"A¹"

1. News -   spread quick —— to   both —— young and old -
2. That's   the   dance   of   Vlad   the   knigh -   t

1. Brave —— dancing   knight —— that was the   stor-y   told !
2. Now   you can see   why   he didn't have to   figh -   t

too - doodle   oodle oodle   oo —— the   trum —— pets would play

Twirling and a twirling and a twirling and a twirling   Vladimir —— would say   Hey!

70

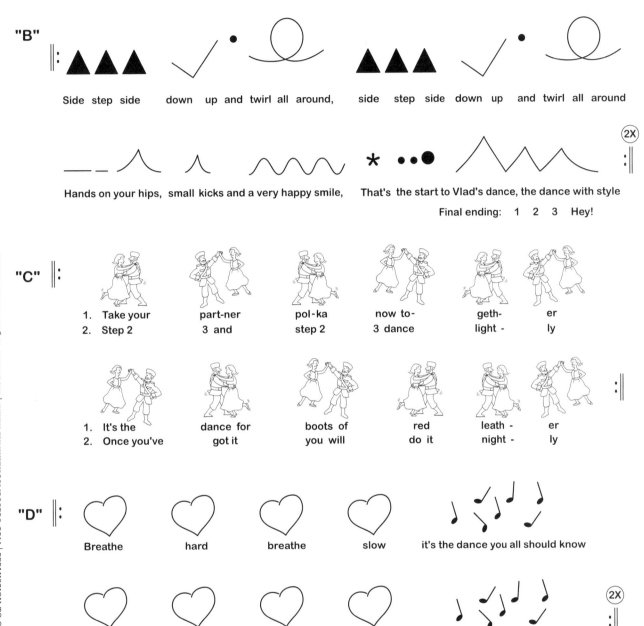

"B"

Side step side   down up and twirl all around,   side step side down up and twirl all around

Hands on your hips, small kicks and a very happy smile,   That's the start to Vlad's dance, the dance with style

(2X)

Final ending: 1 2 3 Hey!

"C"

1. Take your   part-ner   pol-ka   now to-   geth-   er
2. Step 2   3 and   step 2   3 dance   light -   ly

1. It's the   dance for   boots of   red   leath -   er
2. Once you've   got it   you will   do it   night -   ly

"D"

Breathe   hard   breathe   slow   it's the dance you all should know

Breathe   hard   breathe   slow   one more time before we go.

(2X)

Repeat from A¹

Final Form: A B C D A¹ B

Hungarian Dance no. 5

MUSIC: J. BRAHMS; ARR./LYRICS: D. ZIOLKOSKI

* Written music may differ from CD recording, as a few sections were transposed up an octave to better suit the child's vocal range

Final form: A B C D A B

Hungarian Dance no. 5
MUSIC: JOHANN BRAHMS

Goal
To familiarize the students with "Hungarian Dance no. 5" by Johann Brahms. Students will be able to recognize the form of the music, sing and dance along to the orchestration and add in various non-pitched percussion instruments as accompaniment.

Related Concepts
Phrasing, mirroring, light vs. heavy sound qualities.

Recommended Grade: grade 2+

Suggested Themes
Medieval knights.

Materials required
CD, music map, non-pitched percussion instruments (optional).

Vladimir, the King's Favourite Knight

Hundreds of years ago, in the time of Robin Hood, there was a very rich king who lived high up on a hill. He was a gentle, kind, king who was usually very happy.

He shared his riches with others, but for some this was not enough! There were lots of sneaky thieves in the countryside who desperately wanted to get their hands on the king's fortune.

Fortunately, the king was a very smart man, and he kept his castle very well protected. Since his castle was so high on the hill, his guards could see the enemy approaching from miles and miles away. Even when the enemy did manage to get near the castle, they were faced with a second very tricky dilemma: the dreaded moat!

This was no ordinary moat! This was a moat that was filled with mean alligators and icky, gross, slime. No thief would ever want to end up in this moat. Ick!

This did not keep them from trying, though. Every so often, a thief did manage to get across.

Sometimes, they crossed by using a sneaky kind of spy boat, other times by hanging onto the drawbridge when it was lowered for the king to cross.

When the thieves did get across, the king never had to worry, because he always had his favourite knight, Vladimir. Vladimir wasn't your typical type of knight. He didn't wear a suit of armour; he wore his best dancing suit. He had on a furry black hat, a loose white blouse, blue baggy pants, and the most important item of all—his red dancing boots.

Vladimir wasn't a fighting knight. He was a dancing knight! Like the king, he never wanted to really hurt anyone. He would just give them a bit of a scare and send them back to where they were supposed to be.

He would simply fling his hands, and give high kicks and twirls with his red dancing boots, and the next thing you knew, the enemies were tumbling down the hill right into the moat!

It didn't matter how many enemies tried to approach Vladimir at once, for he was such a quick and fancy dancer that he could send as many as ten thieves flying with one graceful kick!

As you can imagine, Vladimir's fame spread quickly. News spread swiftly to both young and old, and soon thousands of people from all around would watch in the forests nearby to see Vladimir dance to protect the castle.

Those thieves that did try to fight with Vladimir only did so once, for every single one of them ended up in the slimy, icky moat. They were much too scared to ever try again.

Vladimir became the most famous dancing knight ever to have lived in medieval times. If you listen closely to his song you will hear which magical steps he took to protect the king and then you too can join him in his dance!

Lesson One

Objective
To read the story, and teach Sections A and B.

Suggested Teaching Process
Section A
- Read students the story.
- Ask students if they would like to learn this dance. Invite them onto the floor, asking them to scatter around the room.
- Ask the students to listen as you play the marching stimuli on the hand drum. Ask them to move as they see fit. (Look for students marching, and positively reinforce them so that all students begin to do the same.)
- Indicate a change in direction by adding a quick tap of the hand drum before the eighth beat. Inform students that this quick tap is a cue to switch directions. Practice playing the eight-beat pattern with this additional quick tap a few times as students practice switching directions after each cue.
- Ask the students to march right, and then move to the left on the sound cue.
- Sing Section A's lyrics for the students. Ask them to echo you back as you sing Section A to them phrase by phrase.
- When the lyrics and melody line are secure for this part, ask them to listen as you sing Section A through while lightly playing the first sixteen beats on the hand drum. (Remember to add in the light tap before the first eighth beat so students will be reminded to switch directions.) Tell students that while you sing, they should be visualizing how to move to this part.
- With you playing the hand drum to the marching stimuli (for the first sixteen beats only), ask students to move as they visualized to Section A while singing the suggested lyrics. Join the students the second time, adding in the simple actions that occur immediately after the word "fight" in phrase two. (Refer to "Suggested Actions" at the end of the lesson)

Section B
- Ask students to remain on the floor, as you once again play the marching stimuli. Can they march side ways? How? (Side step, side step, etc.) Reinforce the side step combination by asking student volunteers to demonstrate for the class.
- Holding a guiro in a vertical position. Demonstrate playing it down-up. Ask students how they might use their bodies to imitate that sound.

- Can they move down-up while keeping their feet glued to the ground? (Remaining stationary.)
- Ask students if they can move down-up one more time, but this time adding a kick with one of their legs when they are moving up (almost like a down-kick).
- Have students listen while trying to visualize the movements as you sing aloud, "Side-step-side, down-up and twirl all around." (Refer to music for the melody line.) Sing this part twice, giving students time to really think about what this might look like. Ask for student volunteers to demonstrate their movement thoughts. Try guiding students towards the recommended actions for this part.
- Demonstrate for the students, asking them to sing along with you as you perform this part. Ask the students to join you the second time through.
- Ask students to listen as you sing the final two phrases of Section B. "Hands on your hips, small kicks and a very happy smile. That's the start to Vlad's dance, the dance with style!" Once again, ask if there are any students who could volunteer what this might look like. Demonstrate for the students, having them join in the second time through.

Section C
- In Section C you will have to spend some extra time teaching the polka step. Slowly demonstrate this step to the students. (Side-step- right, bring your left foot next to your right and lightly shift your weight over for a gentle touch down of your left foot. Transfer your weight back to the right foot.)
- Ask students to mirror you; stand where they can all see you.

Polka Step:
Movement words you could say aloud to assist the students are: right, left, right; or right, touch, right. Practice moving in both directions, with a left, right, left; or left, touch, left. When the students are secure in this, begin on the right foot, and you will naturally start the second polka step (combination of three moves) on the left foot.

If you prefer to stay away from specific feet, you might just like to say, "Step, 2, 3." If the students are not able to do this step, keep it positive and encourage them, even if all they are doing is moving in the same general direction. Remember, keep it fun and simple!

- Gradually increase your speed. Use the hand drum to help the students hear the difference between the "step" (on the skin) and the light "touch down" of the other foot (on the rim), back to the "step" on the rim. (Play skin-rim-skin, accenting the first beat.) Discuss how this step is similar to the waltz step. (The waltz step is step-toe-toe, while the polka step is step-toe-step. The polka step is bouncier in nature, with more of an accent on beats one and three.)
- If the students are having difficulties with this step, invite them to work in partners. To facilitate this, ask the students to form two parallel lines, with partner #1 (they choose) in one line, and partner #2 facing them. Ask partner #1's to begin as together you mirror the polka step to partner #2. After students have tried this a few times, switch turns having partner #2's lead by mirroring for partner #1's.
- When students are able to polka at a fairly quick pace, demonstrate this section as you sing aloud. Use a student volunteer to act as your partner.

This is a very difficult step, so if students are not able to do the step, don't worry. I find that signaling to students by waving my hand high in the air in the direction that they should be moving really helps!

- Demonstrate the movements of the entire Section C for the students as you sing aloud. Teach the melody for this section. When the melody is secure, ask the students to move along with you the second time as you sing and dance through Section C.
- Try Section C with the recording. Use this time as an opportunity to reinforce the terms vivace (very fast), poco rit (slow down a little), and in tempo (return to original tempo).
- The music then returns to Section A, with a variation in the words. Teach students the new lyrics by rote, and when they are secure with them, sing and dance through the piece in its entirety. I suggest that the first time you simply sing and dance through it at your own pace; the

second time use the CD (which will more than likely have a faster tempo than you originally practiced).

Lesson Two

Objective
To review by singing and dancing through the entire selection. To conduct through the music map, and add in non-pitched percussion accompaniment (optional).

Suggested Teaching Process
Review once through "Hungarian Dance no. 5" (using the CD), with the movement and lyrics learned in the previous lesson. Once the students' memories are refreshed, continue with the outline below.

Introduce the music map
- Have the students join you in front of the large music map. While listening to the CD, review through the entire selection.
- Conduct the class music map as students conduct in the air using their conducting finger.
- Ask one volunteer who was accurately following the music map to guest conduct. (Remember the top hat and special conducting baton.)

Suggested Instrumentation for Section B
1. Claves: side-step-side
2. Guiro: down-up
3. Maracas: and twirl all around
4. Tambourine: 1, 2, 3, Hey! (On the word "Hey" can hold the tambourine high up in the air and give one great shake.)

Summary of Suggested Movements/Actions

Section A:

- Vladimir the king's favourite knight: *March right with hands on hips.*
- Learned how to dance, others just learned to fight: *March left, hands on hips.*
- Great men would fall with one graceful kick: *Hand straight in front, moving outwards in one smooth motion. Index finger indicates the word "one."*
- Tumbling and tumbling…into the moat so thick: *Quick rolling motion with arms placed in front of chest.*
- Ick: *Plug nose.*
- News spread quick to both young and old: *Whisper action first to the right and then to the left (on words "news" and "both").*
- Brave dancing knight: *Hands proudly stretched outward.*
- That was the story told: *Shake finger, other hand on hip.*
- Too toodle oodle oodle oo the trumpets would play: *Pretend to play the trumpet.*
- Twirling and a-twirling: *Twirling motion with hands held high up.*
- Vladimir would say, "Hey!": *Hands high up in the air.*

Section B

- Side step side: *Right close right.*
- Down up and twirl all around: *Plié down. When coming up, have left leg give a small kick outwards, then twirl once around with hands out. Repeat.*
- Hands on your hips, small kicks, and a very happy smile: *Place one hand on the hip on the word "hands," and then the other hand on the hip on the word "hips." Give small straight kicks outwards.*
- That's the start to Vlad's dance, the dance with style: *Hands on hips.*

Repeat entire Section B.

Section C

- Take your partner; polka now together: *Take the person to your right, one hand on their shoulder, the other holding the person's hand. (Or just by holding each other's hands while standing across from them.) Perform the polka step to pulse. (Three times.)*
- It's the dance of boots of red leather: *Continue as above.*
- Step-2-3, and step-2-3, dance lightly: *Continue as above.*
- Once you've got it you will do it nightly: *Continue as above.*

Section D

- Breathe hard, breathe slow: *Stop, and just sing while catching breath.*
- It's the dance you all should know: *Polka to pulse (two times).*
- Breathe hard, breathe slow: *Stop, catch your breath.*
- One more time before we go: *Polka to pulse (two times).*

Section A1

- That's the dance of Vlad, the knight: *March right, hands on hips.*
- Now you can see why he didn't have to fight: *March left, hands on hips.*
- Too toodle oodle oodle oo the trumpets would play: *Pretend to play the trumpet.*
- Twirling and a-twirling…: *Twirling motion with hands held high up.*
- Vladimir would say, "Hey!": *Hands high up in the air.*

Section B

Same as above, but add in special ending, "1, 2, 3, Hey!"

Final Form: A B C D A1 B

Habanera
MUSIC: G. BIZET; MUSIC MAP: D. ZIOLKOSKI

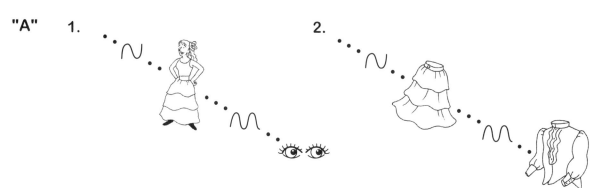

Look   at   me,   a   true   gyp-sy,   Car-men's   my   name   watch   out!

"A"   1.      2.

1. There you stand tall and look at me, you seem not interested we shall see

2. I'll toss my hair and I'll swing my skirt, I'll steal your Heart and lead you by the shirt!

1.   2.

1. I am strong and I need you not, you weave your web but I will not get caught!

2. My knees shake and I feel your power, Micaela's a memory from this hour!

"B"

We have fun, Oh we like to tease,   The crowd cheers on, Oh how we like to   please

They don't know that it's just a game,   that's brought us fortune   and so much fame!

"C"

Jo - sé has stirred my gypsy heart, I toss my flower then I turn to part!

she takes my hand I meet her glance, we then get ready for a spec - ial dance!

"D"

Step strong and sharp and tip toe back, now circle round and do not make a sound

Step strong and sharp and tip toe back, just one more dance will send them in a trance

"C"

Jo - sé has stirred my gypsy heart, I toss my flower then I turn to part!

she takes my hand I meet her glance, we then get ready for a spec - ial dance!

"D"

Step strong and sharp and tip toe back, now circle round and do not make a sound

Step strong and sharp and tip toe back, and take a deep bow then we'll say olé, o-lé!

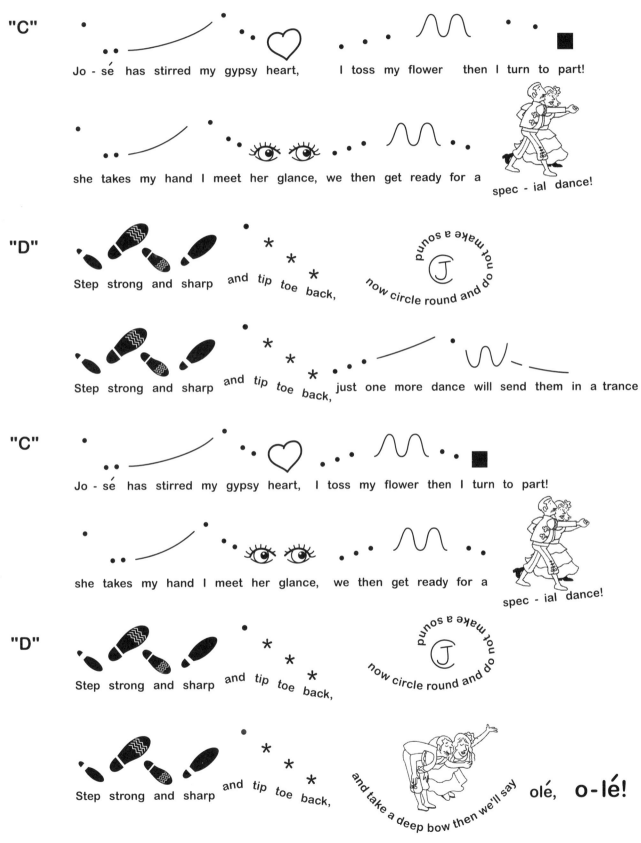

Habanera

MUSIC: G. BIZET; ARR./LYRICS: D. ZIOLKOSKI

Habanera

MUSIC: GEORGES BIZET

Goal
To familiarize students with "Habanera" from the Opera, *Carmen*. Students will sing, dance, and play through this selection.

Related Concepts
Term "opera", melody line on the soprano recorder.

Materials required
CD, music map, soprano recorder (optional).

Lesson One

Objective
To teach Section A of "Habanera." Students will sing, dance and conduct through this section.

Suggested Teaching Process
- Discuss the term opera with students. Explain how it is a story that is sung, either comic or tragic. The story includes scenery, acting, and the accompaniment of an orchestra.
- Read the opera synopsis together as a class (refer to "Carmen" on page 97). Discuss some of the more obvious character traits of José and Carmen. Record these on the board (José was jealous, possessive, proud and stubborn. Carmen was vain, seductive, dishonest and aggressive.)
- Explain to students that "Habanera" was known as a love song in the opera, *Carmen*. Play students the instrumental version. Have they heard it before?
- Tell students that you will play it again, but this time with fun words which were written to help students remember important points about the story. The original words were sung in French, and were very different than the ones that they are about to hear.

Sing/Act/ Play through Section A
- Demonstrate the actions for the students while playing the version of the music which contains the lyrics. Show students parts belonging to both Carmen and José, adding extra drama to make it exciting and fun.
- Teach students the lyrics to Section A, having them echo you phrase by phrase. When the melody line is secure, invite students onto the floor and work through the suggested actions/ movements. Have students act out both sections with you.
- To reinforce lyrics and actions, randomly divide the class into two, asking one half of the class to act as José and the other half to act as Carmen. Tell students to keep their eyes on you, as you will be demonstrating both parts.
- Switch parts. Practice using the recording with the lyrics.
- Ask students to find a partner. Designate one person as José and the other as Carmen. (By designating roles, the pressure is taken off the students if it is two females, or two males working together.) Switch parts.

If the students have their own movement/action ideas for this section, feel free to adapt and incorporate them in.

Introduce the music map
- After the lyrics and actions are fairly secure, ask students to take a seat near the music map. Play through the lyrical version of Section A of "Habanera," asking students to follow along on the music map.
- Play the instrumental version for the students, asking them to conduct along in the air as you guide them through Section A of the music map.
- Ask volunteers to come and conduct on the class-sized map, while others conduct along in the air.

Lesson Two

Objective
To teach Sections B and C of "Habanera." Review it in its entirety.

Suggested Teaching Process
- With the assistance of the lyrical accompaniment, sing/act through Sections A and B.

- Explain to students that in Section B the true feelings of the actors who play these parts are revealed. They are amused with the popularity of the characters they portray to the audience, and are thrilled with the fame that the role is bringing them.
- Ask students to listen as you sing/move through this section that the actors sing in unison. Demonstrate the suggested movement with the help of a volunteer. Sharply strut around in a small circle to the beat of the music. Swiftly change directions at the end of the phrase to make it dramatic and humorous for the students.
- Teach students the melody by rote, and invite them to join you as you work through the movement together. Have students work individually, and then, when they are comfortable with the movements, ask them to find a partner. Exaggerate the movements/actions so the students feel comfortable and find it a humorous exercise.
- Teach Section C using the same process. Be very dramatic when demonstrating the sharp tango-style step while strutting to the lyrics "step strong and sharp, and gently back."
- When you have worked through all the sections, review from the beginning using the lyrical accompaniment the first time through. You may like to randomly divide the class into halves, designating one half as the "Josés" and the other as the "Carmens."
- To keep it organized, I find having the "Josés" in one line with the "Carmen" partners close on their right, helps students remember which part they are singing.
- Practice with the music. (Both versions if time permits.)

Introduce Section B and C of the music map
- Invite students to take a seat near the class-sized music map. With the assistance of the music, conduct through the music together.
- Ask students to conduct in the air as you guide them through the map.
- Invite students who are confident with their ability to follow the map, to guide the class through the class-sized music map as others conduct in the air.

Lesson Three

Objective
To review listening questions together. Discuss/review instruments of the orchestra (optional). To discuss dynamics and form of the music.

Suggested Teaching Process
- Review through the class-sized music map together. Ask students if they know what the form (order) of the music is?
- Ask students to take a pencil and paper, and record the form/order of the piece as you play the CD (either version). Compare answers, and then listen to the music together, and ask the students to assist you as you record the form on the board while the music plays. (Final form: Intro. A B C C)

Review through the following listening questions together:

Suggested Listening Questions
1. Listen to the introduction of "Habanera." What stringed instrument can play at such a low register? (The double bass.)
2. Is the introduction being bowed or plucked? (Bowed.)
3. What would the difference in sound be between bowed notes and plucked noted? (Bowed notes are generally smooth, and plucked notes sound more detached.)
4. What happens to the dynamic level in Section C? (Dynamics change from fortissimo {loud} to piano {soft}.)
5. Were the dynamics effective in expressing the love story that Bizet may have wanted to relay between his characters José and Carmen? (Yes.) If so, what emotion might the loud sections have represented? (Anger, jealousy.) Discuss this with the students.
6. After the double bass introduces the piece, the violins enter, representing Carmen's voice. At what point do you hear the introduction of a special wind instrument? (Section A for José's singing part.) What is the name of this wind instrument? (Oboe.)

7. Which instrument is introduced in Section B and is very unique in sound? (The bells.) Does this add to the playful character of this section? (Yes.)

8. The bells play a rhythmic pattern similar to that of another instrument. Which instrument is this? (The double bass.)

If time permits, review the music in its entirety, singing/dancing and acting through the sections.

Summary of Suggested Movements/Actions

Section A
Introduction
Measures 1–4: Carmen sings to José
- "Look at me, a true gypsy, Carmen's my name. Watch out." *On "Look" one hand on own hip with the other hand's thumb tapping chest. Stand very proud, demanding attention.*

Measures 5–8
- "There you stand tall and look at me." *Strut four steps forward bringing the same shoulder as foot forward to accentuate the beat.*
- "You seem not interested; we shall see." *Stand still shaking finger, then nodding smugly on "We shall see."*
- "I'll toss my hair and I'll swing my skirt, I'll steal your heart and lead you by the shirt." *Carmen walks to the beat, circling around José, tossing her hair and swinging her hips (in an exaggerated way). On "I'll steal your heart" tap thumb on own chest on the word "I," and then put hand on chest on the word "heart." On the word "shirt," tap José's shirt firmly with index finger.*

Measures 13–16: José sings to Carmen
- "I am strong and I need you not." *José brings arms up to flex muscles and then on "I need you not" pretends to shoo her away turning his head briskly on the word "not."*

Measures 17–20
- "My knees shake and I feel your power, Micaela's a memory from this hour." *Exaggerate shaking knees to the beat. On the word Micaela, twirl finger in a circular motion on the side of your head in a "crazy" gesture. On the word "memory," shrug shoulders as if to say "Micaela who?"*

Section B: Carmen and José sing/dance together
Measures 21–24, and 25–28
- "We have fun; oh, we like to tease. The crowd cheers on; oh, how we like to please. They don't know that its just a game that's brought us fortune and so much fame." *Holding partner's hands with one elbow bent and the other straight, with both people facing in the same direction (tango style), strut around in a small circle to the beat of the music. At the end of the phrase, abruptly change directions and strut around the other way.*

Section C: Carmen sings to José
Measures 29–32
- "José has stirred my gypsy heart; I toss my flower, then I turn to part." *Stand still while crossing hands on your heart. On "toss" pretend to toss flower down at partner's feet, and on "part" briskly turn your head in the other direction.*

Measures 33–36: José sings to Carmen
- "She takes my hand, I meet her glance, we then get ready for a special dance." *Take hands, pull each other eye to eye (exaggerate this for comic relief), on "we then get ready," partners get into the tango position, both facing the same direction, both bodies getting ready to take sharp steps.*

Section D: Carmen and José sing/dance together
Measures 37–40
- "Step strong and sharp, and tip toe back; now circle 'round and do not make a sound." *In tango position with bodies facing the same direction, one hand around waists and the other directly out together, step extremely sharply on the words "strong" and "sharp" then on "tip" and "back" go as quietly back as possible. Keep your tango position, tiptoe 'round together with straight arms leading you around, and your feet almost tiptoeing on the spot.*

Measures 41–44
- "Just one more dance will send them in a trance." *Sing out looking at each other smugly.*

Repeat movements from measure 29 until the last measure of "and take a deep bow." Here, bow to each other in a fancy way, then on the first "Olé" put hands on hips, and on the second "Olé," throw them fiercely into the air shouting "Olé!".

Remember these are just suggestions. Feel free to adapt them to reflect your own teaching style. Have fun!

Lessons Four, Five, Six: Recorder Challenge

Objective
To introduce the melody line of "Habanera" on the soprano recorder. *It is strongly recommended that students have at least two years recorder experience before attempting this lesson.*

Materials required
A large visual of the melody line, and simple drawings of the recorders indicating how to play notes low D through high D (including F#, G#, A#/B flat, high C#).
*Refer to a soprano recorder book for the notes.

Suggested Teaching Process
With a large visual of the melody line at hand, review through the notes starting with the low D, working your way up the D major scale (F# and C#).

When the students are secure with this, introduce them to G#, B flat, and high C#. Practice using various four-beat echo patterns.

Take extra time in reviewing the correct way to hold and play the recorder (hold it at a forty-five degree angle, elbows comfortably out, back straight, and thinking of the word "doo" when blowing gently in your recorder.)

When students are sufficiently warmed up, begin playing very small segments of the piece, having the students echo them back. Work through the melody line, taking time to sing through the notes and playing fun games which involve the students searching for small segments which you play.

Ask various students to come up and conduct through the music, while others play. Try to use various teaching techniques to hold the students' interest.

Provide students with a copy of the music, asking them to practice for at least ten to fifteen minutes at home.

As Section C has fewer accidentals, you may wish to begin teaching this section first. When's children feel secure and confident with this section, teach section A. All classes/students levels are different. Remember to adapt to your students' needs.

Composer Biographies
&
Activity Sheets

Wolfgang Amadeus Mozart

Wolfgang Amadeus Mozart
(1756-1791)

Wolfgang Amadeus Mozart was born in Salzburg, Austria, in 1756. The Mozart house was a very musical one. Wolfgang's father, Leopold Mozart, was a composer and a violinist.

When Wolfgang's sister, Nannerl, was seven, she began lessons on the clavier (a small keyboard). Wolfgang's father let him listen to her lessons while he played, but always told him that he was too little to take lessons himself.

One day, however, Mozart played one of his sister's pieces without ever having taken a single lesson! By the age of four he could play anything his sister played, and also compose music of his own. Wolfgang also became an excellent violinist. Without having taken even one lesson, he picked up the violin and played it like an expert. He was an amazing little boy.

Wolfgang's father planned a tour with both his children. Wolfgang and his sister performed together, charming everyone in the land. They were even invited to play for the king and queen! Mozart was especially talented and charming. He had a great sense of humour, and loved making people laugh!

One day, while giving a concert for the king, Mozart played so well that the king thought he was tricking him. The king didn't believe it was possible for such a young child to play so well. So, right before Mozart was about to play the clavier, the king pulled out a black cloth and placed it over the keyboard so that Mozart couldn't see the keys. Then he asked Mozart to play.

Mozart just laughed, since it didn't make any difference to him whether the keys were covered or not. He started to play, and he played his piece perfectly, without missing a note! The king couldn't believe it!

When Mozart grew older, people didn't seem to find him so cute anymore. They got used to him composing such amazing music, so many of them stopped going to his concerts, and he became quite poor.

Mozart had great parties and bought many beautiful clothes, but he often forgot to save for important things! When he was just thirty-five years old, Mozart got very sick and died. There was no money for a funeral or a cross for his grave, but many years later the people of Vienna built a great monument in his memory.

Today, Mozart is still one of the greatest musicians ever to have lived! People from all over the world listen to and love his music.

Johann Strauss

Johann Strauss II

(1825-1899)

Johann Strauss II was born in Vienna, Austria in 1825. He had two younger brothers, a kind mother, and a father who was a professional musician.

When Johann was just a little boy, he loved music and was very interested in it. His father, however, didn't want any of his children to be musicians, as he believed they would be much better off if they became bankers.

Johann and his brothers begged their mom (who knew how to play piano) to give them music lessons. Johann's mom knew that her boys wanted music lessons very badly. After some thought, she decided to teach the children piano lessons herself. They kept these lessons a secret from Mr. Strauss.

Johann also had a love for the violin, so, with the help of his mother, he secretly took violin lessons and paid for them himself with money that he made through teaching music lessons to a neighboring tailor.

One day, while Johann was practicing the piano, his father who had been away at work, popped into the house to pick up something he had forgotten. When he walked into his house, he was shocked to see Johann playing the piano so well. He didn't even know that he knew how to play.

His father was very angry! He was so furious that his children had learned music without his permission and that everyone had kept this a secret from him, that he packed his bags and left the house.

When Johann grew older, he still followed his father's wishes by going to school to learn how to be a banker. But as soon as he did this, Johann decided he needed to follow his heart and study music.

Like his dad, Johann began writing great dance music. He composed hundreds of dance selections including waltzes, polkas, and marches. With the help of his brothers, Strauss organized and conducted many orchestras all around Austria. Everyone's favourite piece was "The Blue Danube" waltz! Soon people were calling Johann the "waltz king," a title once given to his father.

His father was not happy about this, and even stopped talking to his son for a while. Johann was very well liked though, and had many great friends. He was good friends with Johannes Brahms, another famous composer and musician of his time.

Camille Saint-Saëns

Camille Saint-Saëns

(1835-1921)

Camille Saint-Saëns was born in Paris, France, almost two hundred years ago. Shortly after he was born, his father died. His mother and his great aunt took on the great job of raising the little boy.

Camille was a very smart toddler, and by the age of three, he was able to read and write. His mom and his great aunt worked very hard with him, teaching him piano. By the time Camille was five, he was ready to give his first piano concert. By the time he was seven he began composing music.

When he was a teenager, Camille went to study music at a famous music school in Paris. Everyone thought he was a great organist, but soon they began to realize that Camille was also a very talented composer. He wrote his first symphony when he was just sixteen years old!

As Camille grew older, he became very popular, especially when he conducted the orchestra that played his music.

When he turned forty, Camille got married to a lady who was only twenty. They had two young boys, but had very terrible luck. Their first son got very sick and died, and just six weeks later their other son fell out of an open window and died. Camille and his wife were very depressed and upset about their children's deaths, and decided to go their separate ways.

Even though Camille had some very difficult times, he still managed to have a sense of humour. He liked to show off his sense of humour in his music. He did so with one of his most famous works ever, the "Carnival of the Animals."

After Camille wrote this music, he hid it high up in his closet. He only allowed one of the pieces from this collection to be played, because it was more serious than the rest. It was called "The Swan" and was written especially for the cello. It was a beautiful piece that everyone loved.

During his life, Saint-Saëns wrote over three hundred works, including thirteen operas. Camille Saint-Saëns was also the first composer to ever write music for the cinema. When he died, he was eighty-six years old.

Soon after his death, one of Camille's friends found "Carnival of the Animals" hidden in his closet, and published it for the world to hear. Everyone loved this music, and Saint-Saëns became even more famous, even after his death.

Edvard Grieg

Edvard Grieg

(1843-1907)

Grieg was born in Bergen, Norway. His father was a merchant and his mother a very talented pianist. There were five children in Grieg's family; Grieg was the fourth child. His mother gave him piano lessons when he was six years old, and after years of practice a family friend noticed that young Grieg was very talented and recommended that he go to a special music school called the "Leipzig Conservatory." Grieg was just 15 years old when he joined this school.

A few years later when Grieg was 17 years old, he became very sick with pleurisy, a disease that affects your lungs. This disease bothered Grieg for the rest of his life. After Grieg graduated, he traveled in Denmark where he met other Norwegian composers.

One of the young composers whom he met on his travels, convinced him that he should try writing a symphony. When Grieg finished his symphony, he was not happy with it. He decided that he didn't want anyone to hear it, so he instructed that it never be played in public.

When Grieg was a bit older, he decided that he wanted to stay in Norway to write music that was influenced by Norwegian folk songs. Grieg married his cousin Nina who was a talented singer. They had one daughter Alexandra who died when she was very young.

Grieg continued composing many wonderful pieces, and became very famous for pieces called, "Peer Gynt" and "Norwegian Dances." Grieg spent his last years of his life traveling giving concerts with his wife. He had a happy life and was loved by many.

Johannes Brahms

Johannes Brahms

(1833-1897)

Johannes Brahms was born in Hamburg, Germany six short years after Beethoven died. Brahms began learning how to play the piano when he was five years old, being taught by his father who was a musician.

His father realized that Brahms had a natural talent for the piano, since he knew the names of all the keys before even taking a single lesson. Brahms' father soon had him playing in local taverns and inns, earning money to help support the family. This came to an end when Brahms gave his first public piano concert when he was ten years old.

A well-respected teacher and composer heard Brahms play, and agreed to teach him piano. Brahms worked very hard, and progressed quickly.

He loved playing pieces composed by Bach and Beethoven.

Brahms was a very quiet, shy young boy who preferred to be by himself. When he twenty, he was introduced to Franz Liszt, another great composer and musician. At first, Liszt was impressed by Brahms, but soon lost interest when Brahms fell asleep while Liszt was playing for him. Liszt was very insulted by this.

Brahms did not enjoy Liszt's aggressive personality, and found comfort and friendship with Robert and Clara Schumann instead. These three musicians remained friends throughout their lives.

Brahms continued to work hard, conducting, composing and playing throughout Europe. Brahms spent much of his later years in Vienna, Austria where he worked very slowly and meticulously on his compositions.

Sadly, before he died, Brahms destroyed all the music he composed before he was nineteen years of age. He didn't want the world to see anything except perfect scores, which, in his opinion, were just a small portion of the thousands of pieces he composed. Brahms is known to be one of the greatest composers of the Romantic period. Today, one of the most familiar melodies for children is Brahms' Lullaby.

Georges Bizet

Georges Bizet
(1838-1875)

Georges Bizet is best known for his opera, *Carmen*. It is a very spirited opera and is one of the world's favourites. During his short life he wrote many operas, but none thrilled audiences quite like *Carmen*.

Bizet was born into a musical family. His father was a singing teacher and a composer, and his mother a fine pianist. His parents gave him a strong, musical start, and then sent Bizet to the Paris Conservatory when he was nine. At the age of nineteen, he won the Grand Prix de Rome for a cantata, as well as the Prix Offenbach for a comical opera.

The Prix de Rome included winning three years to study in Italy. This was perhaps the happiest time of his life. He loved Italy's people, music, and language.

When he returned to Paris in 1860, Bizet decided to pursue a career in writing operas. Unfortunately he was not very successful. In 1869, he married Genevieve Halevy. He continued writing operas, but also composed three symphonies and many piano compositions.

Bizet spent two months writing the music for the opera *Carmen*. When it was first introduced in Paris in 1875, the audience was appalled, and found many of the scenes shocking and disturbing.

Carmen was played over forty-eight times in Paris, with many of its performances half empty. Towards the last few shows, management had to give away free tickets to fill up the theatre.

Bizet was very depressed after this public reception of his opera in Paris, and died shortly after. After his death, the opera was launched in Vienna and soon became triumphant worldwide. Sadly, he never realized how successful *Carmen* was to become.

Carmen
OPERA/MUSIC: BIZET

Carmen is one of the world's most loved operas. Its main character, Carmen, is a beautiful, spirited gypsy who seems to cast a spell on José, a guard across from the cigarette factory where she works.

At first, José seemed to be the only man not captivated by her gypsy beauty. This intrigued Carmen, who then pursued him. She used her beguiling charms to exchange a glance with José, and then threw him a flower to remind him of her before dashing back to work.

Her beauty haunted José. He struggled between his professed love for Micaela (whom his mother wanted him to marry) and the gypsy siren Carmen.

Just as José was to marry Micaela, he was asked to accompany Carmen to the local prison as she was said to have wounded a fellow worker in a fight.

Carmen convinced José to go dancing with him, and then help her escape. He untied the ropes which were wound around her wrists and she ran off. José was arrested and sent to prison for assisting her in her escape.

When José was released from prison, he found Carmen and realized that she was being pursued by two other men. Zuniger (an officer) and Escamillo (a bull fighter)—both hoping to win her over.

José was very jealous, and although Carmen told him that she was not interested in those other men, he didn't believe her. He then murdered Carmen and her love interest, and was once again arrested and sent to prison.

The Great Escape

HELP THESE AMAZING COMPOSERS FIND CHARACTERS WHO HAVE ESCAPED FROM THEIR MUSIC!

Can you draw a line connecting the missing character to the composer?
Beware! Some composers may have more than one character on the loose!
Can you color the characters when you have captured them all?

Musical Word Search
The Life of Johann Strauss

Can you find these hidden words in the word search below?

Brothers	Waltz King	Vienna	March	Violin	Treble clef
The Blue Danube	Brahms	Mother	Fourteen	Banker	Johann
Operetta					

```
W D A R C K T L M A R C H W I I H L I S T V W E L
B S E O P E R E T T A S E V W L I D I T W E V W A
R E R V W V E I N N A S T E I V W V I O L I N D X
A M O T H E R S W I N N E W S C A L E D T B I O R
H S W A L T Z K I N G W D H K O H B A N K E R R W
M E C T H E B L U E D A N U B E W I S T H O D I R
S O T J B L W O P J O H A N N S I T L W E B I R T
B R O T H E R S T R E B L E C L E F W I T O S H I
F O U R T E E N V I O K N I S W E T V S I O O L I
```

Can you unscramble the letters to come up with titles of Strauss compositions?

shctirt   opkal   rattchs   napsier   charm

_____   _____   _____   _____   _____

Know Your Composers

True or False? How well do you know your composers? Circle the correct answer.

1. Georges Bizet's opera Carmen was a great hit when it was first introduced in Paris in 1875. True or False?

2. Mozart was very wealthy, never having to worry about having enough money to support his family. True or False?

3. Camille Saint-Saëns was able to read and write by the young age of three. True or False?

4. Johann Strauss's father was also a great composer of dance music. True or False?

5. Johann Strauss had two sisters who loved music as well. True or False?

6. "Aquarium"and "Fossils" are two pieces which came from Camille Saint-Saëns' "Carnival of the Animals" collection. True or False?

7. Mozart's "Rondo Alla Turca" has a very slow tempo, which could cause you to fall asleep if you are not careful. True or False?

8. A rondo is a piece of music which has many sections which are often repeated. A B A C A D would be an example. True or False?

9. Johannes Brahms refused to write dance music, because he felt that music should be simply listened to and not danced to. True or False?

10. Mozart died a pauper, at the young age of thirty-five. True or False?

11. "Tritsch Tratsch Polka" is an example of a lullaby. True or False?

12. Johann Strauss was called the "waltz king." True or False?

13. Grieg was born in Paris, France. True or False?

14. "Hungarian Dance no. 5" was composed by Bizet. True or False?

15. Brahms, Bizet, Grieg, Strauss, and Saint-Saëns were all composers of the Romantic period. True or False?

Johann Strauss II
Activity Sheet

To answer the following questions, students will need to have read the biography of Johann Strauss.

1.   When was Strauss born?
     A. 1825
     B. 1925
     C. 1600

2.   Where was Strauss born?
     A. Australia
     B. Austria
     C. Amsterdam

3.   Did Strauss have any brothers or sisters? If so, how many? _____

4.   What did Strauss's father do for a profession? _____

5.   Why didn't Strauss's father want his children to become musicians?

     _____

     _____

     _____

6.   How did Strauss learn piano? _____

7.   Strauss graduated from college with a certificate in _____.

8.   Did he ever use this certificate? _____

9.   Strauss was also known as the "_____ king".

10. Name one piece that Strauss composed. _____

Did you know that a polka is an energetic dance in 2/4 time? Strauss just loved writing music that people could dance to. Waltzes and polkas were some of his favourite dancing music.

Can you draw a picture of Strauss conducting an orchestra while people danced the polka? "Tritsch Tratsch Polka" is still one of people's all-time favourite polkas! Did you know that it means "Chit Chat" polka? How fun!

Georges Bizet
Activity Sheet

To answer the following questions, students will need to have read the biography of Georges Bizet and the summary of his opera, *Carmen*.

1. Bizet's family was a very _____ (7 letters) one. His father was a _____

    teacher and _____. His mother was a fine _____.

2. Bizet was best known for the spirited, colourful opera, _____.

3. Bizet spent the best three years of his life in this country: _____.

4. When he returned to Paris he decided to pursue his career in _____, which at that time seemed to be very unsuccessful.

5. Carmen was first introduced in the city of _____.

6. Audiences found the opera quite _____.

7. Carmen was played over _____ times in Paris.

8. Towards the end, the management had to _____ tickets.

9. Bizet believed his opera to be a _____.

10. At what age did Bizet die? _____

Word Scramble

1. Carmen was a beautiful and spirited SYGYP. _____

2. Carmen was sent to prison after having a HTIFG. _____

3. José was a UDAGR who worked across from the cigarette factory. _____

4. Bizet's ARCNEM is one of the world's most loved operas. _____

5. José helped Carmen to PECEAS before being sent to prison. _____

6. Carmen threw a RLFWOE down at José's feet. _____

7. When Carmen was first introduced in SRPAI audiences. _____

Music Detectives

Can you circle the characters which belong to the music being played?
Listen as your teacher plays a mysterious song. Help your teacher by
being a Music Detective and circling the characters which belong to the music.

A Musical Time Line

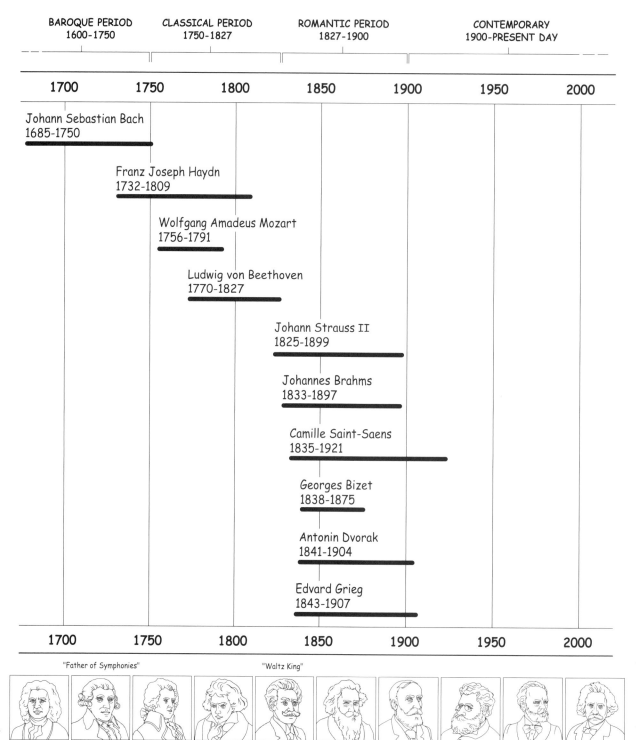

| BAROQUE PERIOD 1600-1750 | CLASSICAL PERIOD 1750-1827 | ROMANTIC PERIOD 1827-1900 | CONTEMPORARY 1900-PRESENT DAY |

1700   1750   1800   1850   1900   1950   2000

Johann Sebastian Bach
1685-1750

Franz Joseph Haydn
1732-1809

Wolfgang Amadeus Mozart
1756-1791

Ludwig von Beethoven
1770-1827

Johann Strauss II
1825-1899

Johannes Brahms
1833-1897

Camille Saint-Saens
1835-1921

Georges Bizet
1838-1875

Antonin Dvorak
1841-1904

Edvard Grieg
1843-1907

1700   1750   1800   1850   1900   1950   2000

"Father of Symphonies"   "Waltz King"

Johann Sebastian Bach | Joseph Haydn | Wolfgang Amadeus Mozart | Ludwig van Beethoven | Johann Strauss II | Johannes Brahms | Camille Saint-Saëns | Georges Bizet | Antonin Dvořák | Edvard Grieg

Symphony Orchestra

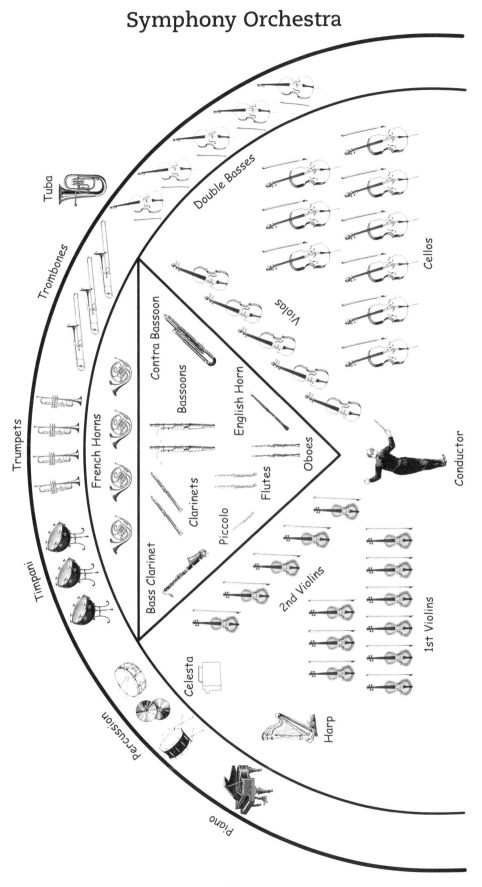

Answer Key

Johann Strauss Activity Sheet

1. 1825
2. Austria
3. Strauss had two brothers
4. He was a professional musician
5. His father didn't think they would earn enough money.
6. His mother secretly taught him piano.
7. He graduated with a certificate in banking.
8. No, he received his certificate but pursued his career as a musician.
9. Waltz King
10. Blue Danube/Tritsch Tratsch Polka/Persian March/Pizzicato Polka

Georges Bizet Activity Sheet

1. musical, his father was a singing teacher and composer, his mother was a fine pianist.
2. Carmen
3. Italy
4. writing operas
5. Paris
6. Appalling
7. 48
8. Give away
9. failure
10. 37

Word Scramble

1. gypsy 2. fight 3. guard 4. Carmen 5. Escape 6. Flower 7. Paris

Music Detective

This is a wonderful evaluation tool. You create your quiz, by playing various excerpts from the CD.

True or False

1. False 2. False 3. True 4. True 5. False 6. True 7. False 8. True 9. False
10. True 11. False 12. True 13. False 14. False 15. True

Fun with Composers brings the great classics to life! The power of storytelling will draw children into the intriguing world of Classical Music!

A Simple, Fun Approach to Classical Music

Storytelling · Drama · Song · Movement · Instrumental Play

Just for Kids Guides *(Ages 3-6) and (Ages 7-12)*

Composer images and stories, music maps, activity pages, intriguing stories and more! A "take-home" version of our Teacher's Guide... made "Just for Kids". Move over Hilary Duff... Mozart and Strauss promise to be the new requested favorites!

Just for Kids Guides (CD included)
$24.95 CDN each
$19.95 US each

"I am a mother of two and have taught Montessori preschool/kindergarten for the past 13 years. I am so excited about the "Fun with Composers" curriculum and have had great success with implementing it in my classroom and also with my own children. The stories and activities are fun, creative and definitely capture a child's attention and imagination! It is a wonderful way to introduce children to classical music in a fun, simple, dynamic manner that is extremely user-friendly! I would recommend this program to all teachers and parents alike. Thank -you for enriching my classroom and helping to instill in both my children an appreciation for classical music! "

With thanks, **Bree Van Ness** *Montessori Training Teacher / Montessori Preschool/Kindergarten Teacher*

Visit our website to place order on-line at www.funwithcomposers.com **or** *Fax or Mail the order form below*

Mail to: *Fun with Composers* 1541 134 A Street, Surrey, B.C. Canada V4A 5P7 **Fax to:** 604-541-2918 **Tel :** 604-541-2928 **Cheques* payable to: "** *Fun with Composers***"**

School:_____ Address:_____ City:_____ State/Prov._____

Code:_____ Telephone: (   )_____ Name of person placing order:_____ Email:_____

Invoice school: _____ or PO#_____ Bill to: *include info on billing if not to the school* _____

Products: Teacher Guides (3-6)_____ (7-12)_____ Just for Kids Guides (3-6)_____ (7-12)_____ **A fee of $25 will be charged for all cheques with insufficient funds*

*GST and PST do not apply. Total $ Amount:_____

Visit our website for all the details! www.funwithcomposers.com

TEACHER'S GUIDES · JUST FOR KIDS GUIDES · CD'S · WORKSHOPS

Fun with Composers

Classical music can come to life through storytelling, drama, creative movement and song. Today, your child was introduced to _____ by _____, a classical composer born over _____ years ago.

Enclosed you will find the story of _____ life, along with his composer image and a music map.

A music map is a child-centered "picture" of the music. It is a combination of squiggles, lines, and markings which are representative of the music. Through the use of the map, your child will be able to follow along with the music and have a better understanding of its form (musical sequence).

If you are interested in purchasing the "Just for Kids" Guidebook/CD which includes all the intriguing stories, music maps, composer activity pages, and a wonderful recording of the music (with lyrics and orchestral arrangement), then please fill out the enclosed order form with cash or a cheque in the amount of $24.95 Cdn, $19.95 US (cheques are payable to "Fun with Composers"). Order forms and payment need to be submitted to _____ no later than _____.

I hope that your child will be interested in sharing his/her musical experience with you to reinforce the learning that occurred in class. Together we will help your child have greater appreciation for one more of the great classics! Enjoy!

Sincerely,

_____

Notes

MUSICAL SEQUENCE

FOR ACCOMPANYING CD

1.	Rondo Alla Turca (Mozart)	3:41	Vocal Performance
2.	Rondo Alla Turca (Mozart)	3:44	Orchestral Arrangement
3.	Tritsch Tratsch Polka (Strauss)	2:48	Vocal Performance
4.	Tritsch Tratsch Polka (Strauss)	2:48	Orchestral Arrangement
5.	Symphony no. 40 (Mozart)	1:53	Vocal Arrangement
6.	Symphony no. 40 (Mozart)	1:51	Orchestral Arrangement
7.	Persian March (Strauss)	1:55	Vocal Performance
8.	Persian March (Strauss)	1:55	Orchestral Arrangement
9.	Fossils (Saint-Saëns)	1:19	Vocal Performance
10.	Fossils (Saint-Saëns)	1:18	Orchestral Arrangement
11.	Aquarium (Saint-Saëns)	2:22	Vocal Performance
12.	Aquarium (Saint-Saëns)	2:22	Orchestral Arrangement
13.	Anitra's Dance (Grieg)	3:21	Vocal Performance
14.	Anitra's Dance (Grieg)	3:23	Orchestral Arrangement
15.	Hungarian Dance no. 5 (Brahms)	2:15	Vocal Performance
16.	Hungarian Dance no. 5 (Brahms)	2:19	Orchestral Arrangement
17.	Habanera (Bizet)	2:04	Vocal Performance
18.	Habanera (Bizet)	2:03	Orchestral Arrangement

Musical recordings under license from Naxos of America. *www.naxos.com*